TOWARD AN AFRICAN FUTURE—
OF THE LIMIT OF WORLD

☰ SUNY SERIES
LITERATURE...IN THEORY

TOWARD AN AFRICAN FUTURE— OF THE LIMIT OF WORLD

NAHUM DIMITRI CHANDLER

SUNY
PRESS

Cover: Photo of W. E. B. Du Bois lecturing on Africa, 1956. The W. E. B. Du Bois Papers (MS 312). Courtesy of the Special Collections and University Archives, University of Massachusetts, Amherst. Cover design by Francis Nunoo-Quarcoo.

Published by State University of New York Press, Albany

For information, contact State University of New York Press, Albany, NY
www.sunypress.edu

Library of Congress Cataloging-in-Publication Data

Name: Chandler, Nahum Dimitri, author.
Title: Toward an African future—of the limit of world / Nahum Dimitri Chandler.
Description: Albany : State University of New York Press, [2021] | Series:
    SUNY series, literature . . . in theory | Includes bibliographical references and
    index.
Identifiers: LCCN 2020040172 (print) | LCCN 2020040173 (ebook) | ISBN
    9781438484198 (hardcover : alk. paper) | ISBN 9781438484181 (pbk. : alk.
    paper) | ISBN 9781438484204 (ebook)
Subjects: LCSH: Du Bois, W. E. B. (William Edward Burghardt),
    1868–1963—Criticism and interpretation. | Du Bois, W. E. B. (William
    Edward Burghardt), 1868–1963. Color and democracy. | Du Bois, W. E. B.
    (William Edward Burghardt), 1868–1963. World and Africa. | American
    literature—African American authors—History and criticism. | Critical theory—
    United States—20th century. | Historiography—United States. | Imperialism—
    Historiography. | Race relations—History. | Africa—Historiography.
Classification: LCC PS3507.U147 Z56 2021 (print) | LCC PS3507.U147 (ebook) |
    DDC 960—dc23
LC record available at https://lccn.loc.gov/2020040172
LC ebook record available at https://lccn.loc.gov/2020040173

10 9 8 7 6 5 4 3 2 1

For Nancy Tierney
(1955–2000)
am memoriam.
She understood the meaning of being black/Black
at the dawning of the twenty-first century.

Contents

Acknowledgments

This text has been presented in several contexts. Two symposia at Queen Mary, University of London (sponsored by way of support from the School of Business and Management at Queen Mary) sparked its present form: most recently, "Historiographies and Cartographies of Global Capitalism–Labour," October 13–15, 2011 (organized under the auspices of the Centre for Ethics and Politics [CfEP] at Queen Mary, by its director, Denise Ferreira da Silva, whom I thank; in the event, David Lloyd and Nicholas De Genova's respective, generous, engagements led me to attempt to render more clearly the terms of my proposed intervention); and earlier, "Post-Colonial Capitalism: A Two-Day Symposium," held at the Goodenough Club, London, on October 15–16, 2009 (organized by Stefano Harney, then of Queen Mary, University of London and Miguel Mellino, of Università degli Studi di Napoli, L'Orientale). In addition, I am grateful for the engagement of my fellow participants during the 2009 session, Denise Ferreira da Silva, Fred Moten, Ranabir Smaddar, and Sandro Mezzadra, for their rich provocations. In addition, sections were presented at the kind invitation of Tsunehiko Kato of Ritsumeikan University (Japan) in his capacity as president of the Japan Black Studies Association (Kokujin Kenkyu no Kai) as part of the plenary symposium "Black Studies in the Age of Globalization" at the 57th annual meeting of the Association in Kyoto, Japan, June 25, 2011. Professor Kato's formulation of the question of the symposium—distributed in written form to both the panelists, which included John McLeod of Leeds University (UK), Amrijit Singh of Ohio University (USA), and Lee Yu-cheng of Academica Sinica (Taiwan), and to the participants in the conference—is a basic reference for the context of my contribution to the symposium. For, my remarks here are offered as one gesture of a potential interlocution. Likewise, some parts of this text in its present form were presented at "An International

Conference: W. E. B. Du Bois and the Question of Another World, II," held on June 6–8, 2007, at the Renaissance Center, located in Shinagawa, Tokyo, under the auspices of the School of Global Studies, both of Tama University. And finally, an earlier formulation of thought was presented at "The Future of Utopia: A Conference in Honor of Fredric Jameson," in the Literature Program at Duke University, April 23–24, 2003. I warmly thank both Prof. Jameson and Prof. Alberto Moreiras, former colleagues and now ongoing friends, for the latter invitation. And then, at the root, the late Yaw Abankwa Manu of Ghana and Yacine Kouyaté of Mali named the voice announced herein and first raised it up for a hearing. My relation to their solidarity is more and deeper than one of gratitude. It is the living of life and death, whatever is such, together. Now, Franc Nunoo-Quarcoo, born of three continents—in the art of his gift of design—must also be announced herein. I thank the editors of *CR: The New Centennial* Review and Michigan State University Press for permission to excerpt passages from texts presented in that journal (6, no. 3 and 12, no. 1). On November 17, 2014, at the UC Riverside, David Lloyd, Jodi Kim, and Ashon Crawley engaged me carefully in faculty seminar. At the University of Oregon, May 4, 2016, Sharon Luk set a touchstone seminar, as Lara Bovilsky, then Joseph Fracchia, each made me welcome. At New York University, October 17, 2018, Annmaria Shimabuku, with Yoon Jeong Oh, allowed this text amplitude as a base for generous discussion. Rashné Limki, of the Living Commons Collective, wonderfully brought Limkigraphics of Mumbai, India, to make possible the 2013 edition, the first, for which I remain profoundly grateful. Cover photo credit: W. E. B. Du Bois, 1956; reproduced from the W. E. B. Du Bois Papers (MS 312), by courtesy of the Special Collections and University Archives, University of Massachusetts Amherst Libraries. For this edition, a salutation to Toumani Diabaté, father, with his son Sidiki, for the elder's composition "Lampedusa," resonant also in "Tunkaranke," both so ancient and so new, across the generations and across the geographies. A faculty publication grant from the University of California, Irvine, Humanities Center graciously supported the publication of the SUNY Press edition of this book. Finally, I thank the scholars and curators, beginning with Prof. H. L. Gates Jr., who made possible the epistemological articulation of the 2017 documentary series *Africa's Great Civilizations*, for it accompanied me during the time of the final preparation of the four annotations added for this edition (McGann 2019).

Preface

This study proposes the value of the presentation of the global level historiographical example in the discourse of W. E. B. Du Bois for theoretical reflection about contemporary historicity. It proceeds first by way of an outline of the catholicity of his engagement with such figures on a worldwide scale of reference. Further, it then explores the question of the place of a certain conception, in which the itinerary of modern slavery is crucial, of the historicity of modern colonialism and its aftermath within Du Bois's thought. The theoretical disposition in question is adumbrated by taking reference to two nodal texts by Du Bois, both of which were issued in the immediate aftermath of the Second World War: *Color and Democracy: Colonies and Peace* (1945) and *The World and Africa: An Inquiry into the Part which Africa Has Played in World History* (1947). Building from a perspective that Du Bois had begun to develop in the closing decade of the nineteenth century, but which he productively elaborated across his entire mature course of thought and practice, those texts fundamentally questioned the dominant premises taking shape to define the post–World War II global order, in particular the Bretton Woods system, at its inception, and delineated a profound sense of the implication—the limits—that it portended for collective forms of human existence for decades, and perhaps centuries, to come. Yet, too, within his octogenarian's sensibility a certain equally profound sense of hope found its way to a renewed kinetic articulation in thought and imagination. For, therein, Du Bois's critical affirmation of the differential articulation of historial profile, beyond the limits of modern colonial horizons or their aftermaths, was otherwise than retrospective. Rather, it was a pragmatic problematization of the past such that its organization could be shown to yield the very terms for the formulation of hope for a future that had not yet shown its face or found its right of historical passage. As such, thinking with Du Bois's initiative in engaging the radical order of the organization of the historial, the name Africa may be adduced as a theoretical metaphor that could propose a certain hyperbolic renarrativization of the systems of modern historicity, not only as pasts, but as futures. In such a path of thought, necessity in the form of a certain finality, even as placed under the mark of death, may well be understood to yet always remain distended in its own possibility. In such a thought, limit can only show by way of its other side: that is, possibility. Limit, approached on the order of necessity itself, if you will, is still, always, thus already a thought of the future as possibility. Such a thought may outline one path to think with and beyond the contemporary forms of the afterlife of modern slavery, colonialism, and imperialism.

For this edition, I have included four annotations: two on the twin major texts noted above, respectively; another on two essays—of the same locution as those two books—written by Du Bois astride the 1940s and the aftermath of the Second World War; and an additional annotation on three major references to music given by Du Bois in his 1945 text. The general bibliographic notation has been revised, as a note on citations.

July 2020

Incipit

If one accepts the epistemic imperatives of the example, its status as an always ensemblic apparition of the supposed proper, and also, thus, its status as a certain order of name for both the limit and the possibility of thought, it might well be engaged as the announcement of an *atopic* order of existence that nonetheless *is*, if you will, only in its immanent appearance: as a site or a seam, an irruption yielded by way of the concatenation that is a fault line; or, as something like the fractual force of waves on the high ocean; or, the terrible heat of a sudden and massive efflorescence, of flame, moving across the desert of the mind's-eye-memory, arising from the sharp and textured frisson of rock against rock; or, according to a distribution of force that takes form, if at all, in the general figure of the cantilever, whether as mountain or bridge.

The *atopic* in this sense is simply an other-than-proper-name of the passage beyond—at the limit of world.

This, if at all, is the fractual immeasurable measure by which we might approach the *question of the utopic* as a matter of existence.

How might such an *anorientation*—that is, a certain tarrying with the intractable character of that which opens the possibility of orientation in general and problematizes in reciprocal fashion, thus that which has often been called the orient in particular—allow us to move with the discourse of one W. E. B. Du Bois in such a manner that it might assist us in thinking through the limit of world—of our sense of world, of this here and this now—toward another passage, other than simply *the* planetary? Perhaps we can accede to its bequest if we accept it as a paradoxical orientation to a problem for thought, as a relation to a practical-theoretical task, as resource for the gathering of our step or gesture in the carriage of the hyperbolic difficulty of theoretical labor in our time, whatever is such. That is to say, in such passage, always within the possibility of, yet always other than, what has been produced by way of a practice under the guidance of the transcendental, there will always have been, examples, perhaps only.[1]

Example

We can open our consideration in medias res, as it were, by reckoning that for Du Bois the Negro American example, incipiting for him as fate or instituted chance, overdetermined in both its freedom and its necessity, posed a question about possibility—ontological and historical, onto-historial—that remained exorbitant for traditional formulations of philosophical question in the modern epoch. The Negro American example, in Du Bois's discourse, is always both and neither, never the simple, always a figure of the double, and never exemplary of the so-called pure, whatever such might be. Thus, from Du Bois's pen comes the inimitable concept-metaphors at the time of the writing of *The Souls of Black Folk* in the years straddling the turn of the twentieth century—"the veil," "double consciousness," "intermingling," "second-sight," "the dawning," "the gift," or even "America," for example. Thus, the question with which he closed that text—one that is itself already a kind of response—could stand as the exemplary form of a world historical question.

> Your country? How came it yours? Before the Pilgrims landed we were here. Here we have brought our three gifts and mingled them with yours: a gift of story and song—soft, stirring melody in an ill-harmonized and unmelodious land; the gift of sweat and brawn to beat back the wilderness, conquer the soil, and lay the foundations of this vast economic empire two hundred years earlier than your weak hands could have done it; the third, a gift of the Spirit. Around us the history of the land has centered for thrice a hundred years; out of the nation's heart we have called all that was best to throttle and subdue all that was worst; fire and blood, prayer and sacrifice, have billowed over

3

this people, and they have found peace only in the altars of the God of Right. Nor has our gift of the Spirit been merely passive. Actively we have woven ourselves with the very warp and woof of this nation,—we fought their battles, shared their sorrow, mingled our blood with theirs, and generation after generation have pleaded with a headstrong, careless people to despise not Justice, Mercy, and Truth, lest the nation be smitten with a curse. Our song, our toil, our cheer, and warning have been given to this nation in blood-brotherhood. Are not these gifts worth the giving? Is not this work and striving? Would America have been America without her Negro people? (Du Bois 1903d, 262–63, chap. 14, para. 25)

To stand with Du Bois in this vocative position shall we say is to exist on both sides of the ostensibly "American" form of limit. In this locution by the narrator of *The Souls of Black Folk*, one must inhabit the problem of existence on both sides of the veil, one must traverse "the veil," and one must render "the veil," all in the same movement of thought and critical discourse. Yet, the movement of Du Bois's practice would accede to an order that is for him even more radical. It might, perhaps, be understood as a certain relation to what has for too long been understood under the heading of death. One must thus also accept the risk of the illimitable as the very configuration of that which one might understand as one's own most belonging: to accede to the limit of possibility and beyond, perhaps, such can only arise as one is truly only always other than oneself. In this sense one only becomes what one is by this carrying forth beyond the limit of (possible) world. Perhaps the name Negro-Colored-Afro-Afra-Black–African American, or even African in this context, is only the name for this tarrying at the threshold at the limit of the impossible possible world.

Let me open the staging of these thetic formulations of a problematization of long-standing within discourse pertaining to matters African American by way of a direct challenge to contemporary theoretical discourse—and such is always *practical* theoretical in its claim—within the various horizons of discussion of modern history, contemporary globalization, and the thought of the postcolonial horizon of our historical present and future.

For what is at stake here is an existential sense and an inner theoretical sense in which no aspect of its possible reference—from which it moves or toward which it moves—is simple. Stated otherwise, its theoretical sense of sight, for example, is always at least—and never only—double. Or, to put

Example   5

it in other terms still, I propose that critical thought more assiduously take resource, implicit or otherwise, in the historically announced plenum for theoretical reflection that Du Bois formulated under the heading of a kind of existential sense of "double consciousness," specifically in its affirmative yield—a kind of "second sight" within and yet beyond the historicity in which it is produced. And, further still, such modes of reflexive and reflective practical-theoretical inhabitation arise as *critical* engagements of that dimension of modern historicity that can be metaphorically nominalized under the heading given by Du Bois as world-historical *problem*—a global level "problem of the color line"—if we understand the sense of problem in his thought to refer to the promulgation of *categorical* forms of proscription, no matter the guise or terms under which such is carried out (the religious, the economic, the so-called racial, the terms of *sex, sexual difference, gender, nationality, citizenship,* etc.). In addition, we can accede to this thought if we also recognize that the term *color* bespeaks not only problem but also possibility—the prospect of new forms and ways for groups of humans to attain or create full realization of historical capacity, or even to open paths toward the possibility of an horizon of unlimited generation and generosity. And, on both levels—of "problem" and "color"—let us here, for the sake of our own historical topos, call it the question of the general necessity and possibility of the migrant (whether forced or unforced, coerced or uncoerced).

To accede to this thought requires the inhabitation of certain "pronounced parallaxes"—never only one. Or, at least this is a register by which one might translate Du Bois's thought of the critical possibilities of "double consciousness," or more properly its yield, "second sight," into vocatives that contemporary critical discourse might find more resonant to its theoretical ear than has been the case up to now—not only in the Americas, north and south, and the Caribbean, or in Europe, but in Asia (remarking Japan as a nodal reference to the announcement of these reflections), and—especially on the horizons of what I am nominalizing herein by way of a paleonymic practice—a certain sense *of* Africa.

We might usefully proceed toward such a proposed interlocution by way of an annotation of the recent accession to a thought of the parallax in certain contemporary critical discourse in and about modern historicity—such as we find it in the deep and inspiring commitment of the relatively recent work of Kōjin Karatani placed under the heading of a "trans-critique" (and also in the various avatars or interlocutions with his formulation of problem). Karatani remarks in his prefatory that his projection is *of* and *from* Japan but not yet so directly *about* Japan, for it follows Karl Marx in the nineteenth-century thinker's "project that elucidates the nature and limit of capital's drive [*Trieb*]" (Karatani 2003, viii). Yet, as a specific production of Karatani's own discourse, his elaboration of the project of a "trans-critique" attains its theoretical opening for the chance of a renewed thought of trans-formation within and perhaps beyond capitalism by way of a reference to the "parallaxes" of reason adduced in the precritical discourse of Immanuel Kant (but a precritical reflection that, in the epistemic sense, was already working over the terrain through which the path to critical thought would later become tractable) (Karatani 2003, viii, 3–4, 30–53).

Yet I propose that Karatani's initiative might find itself rendered more generative still by way of an engagement with the formulation of the prob-lem at stake in Du Bois's discourse and itinerary of practice. Indeed, such resource in interlocution may also enable us to allow Du Bois's thought to take us toward *its* own limit and pose a question that would yet remain beyond such limit as practice.

If this is so—why and how?

In a word, neither proposing nor affirming an accession to a pure term beyond *the movement of* double reference, a radicalization of Du Bois's thought and practice, in part by way of his own example, would affirm the maintenance of such double (or redoubled) movement—a movement of the double—as the very root (if there is such) of critical sense, reflex, judgment, and practical-theoretical intervention. It would be otherwise than the traditional sense of ambivalence; it would be ambivalence with an edge, ambivalence always charged on the bias, of a responsibility for a possible intervention within historicity.

The thought of parallax from which Karatani takes resource is offered in the fourth chapter of Kant's 1766 text *Dreams of a Spirit Seer Elucidated by Dreams of Metaphysics*. The formulations of the status of a parallax in a practice of reason that would be otherwise than naive are produced as the opening and frame of the concluding chapter of the book as a whole and thus remarks on the very opening for thought to which Kant had acceded in the course of that work.

> Scales intended by civil law to be a standard measure in trade, may be shown to be inaccurate if the wares and the weights are made to change pans. The bias [*Parteilichkeit*] of the scales of understanding is revealed by exactly the same strategem [*Kunstgriff*], and in philosophical judgements, too, it would not be possible unless one adopted this strategem, to arrive

Example   7

at a unanimous result [*einstimmiges Fazit*] by comparing the different weighings. . . . I formerly used to regard the human understanding in general merely from the point of view of my own understanding. Now I put myself in the position of someone else's reason which is independent of myself and external to me [*in die Stele einer fremden und äusseren Vernunft*], and regard my judgements, along with their most secret causes, from the point of view of other people. The comparison of the two observations yields, it is true, pronounced parallaxes, but it is also the only method for preventing optical deception, and the only means of placing the concepts in the true positions which they occupy relatively to the cognitive faculty of human nature. . . . But the scales of the understanding are not, after all, wholly impartial. One of the arms which bears the inscription: *Hope for the future*, has a mechanical advantage; and that advantage has the effect that even weak reasons, when placed on the appropriate side of the scales, cause speculations, which are in themselves of greater weight, to rise on the other side. This is the only defect [*Unrichtigkeit*], and it is one which I cannot easily eliminate. Indeed, it is a defect which I cannot even wish to eliminate. (Kant 1992, 336–37)

I leave aside here any attempt to offer the fulsomeness of my engagement with Kant's discourse; and, instead, simply name our recognition of several principal nodes of theoretical reference for Kant's later architectonic as offered by way of this passage. First, Kant's formulation of the first step, or proto-step (in terms of his own itinerary), of a critical practice as "to put myself in the position of someone else's reason" should acquire a highlight here in the context of our proposed interlocution. Second, so too should its implication: "pronounced parallaxes" (which I will translate in a summary manner here as a shift in the appearance of the object by way of shift in the reference according to which the subject can address such an objective, a shifting that then finds no register or generality according to which one position, a supposed singular might be maintained), a proposition to which we might diacritically add the sense of *hue* or *color*. It is always otherwise than the supposed singular. And, third, we annotate—in a manner that we, along with Du Bois, might share with Karatani, Marx, and Kant—that despite all caution, a certain bias will always have remained an ineluctable dimension of *the relation within the movement of parallaxes*, for all forms of judgment are practical-theoretical: they are concerned to determine, *what must be done*, to intervene in the present on behalf of the future.

Perhaps Kant in the critical works sought the resolution of such "pronounced parallaxes" in an attempt to give critical guidance in the negotiation of the "transcendental illusions" produced as "ideas of pure reason" (ideas of—whole or limit, perhaps—which have as such no object for intuition, but appear as necessary for thought—such as *I* or *self, world* or *cosmos*, and *God*; to which I would likely propose we add, for example. *species* and *race*, but that is properly a matter of another scene of interlocution) as remarked in his "Appendix to the Transcendental Dialectic" in the *Critique of Pure Reason* of 1781, and as practiced in both his turning point essay on teleology and the concept of race of 1788 and the exfoliation of the passage within the labor of critical thought according to the latter formulation of the problematic as the *Critique of the Power of Judgment* of 1790 (Kant 1998, 590–623, A642/B670-A704-B732; Kant 2007; Kant 2000).

The track of Karatani's engagement with Kant's formulation here, seems to suggest that for this contemporary thinker the accession to the "unanimous result [*einstimmiges Fazit*]"—as given in the passage quoted above from the eighteenth-century thinker—would not only mark the opening toward the transcendental, and make "us face the problem of universality," but also bequeath access to judgments of such (Karatani 2003, 46–49).

Yet, if Kant's or Karatani's disposition is allowed a reasonable recognition in the recollection that I have given, it can be offered in contradistinction to such a path that having proposed the critical thought of the transcendental and still proceeding by way of its interminable passage, for example the always already given critical recognition that no sense is simple, one must still set afoot or adrift, *always again*, according to a practice that would be—to use an old language, as paleonymy—*ultra-transcendental*: that the transcendental is not, and can never be, a position; or, it is *only* position, always partial and hence nonsimple, and finds its possibility only by way of that which is otherwise and thereby (that is, as always otherwise) allows its articulations (Derrida 1976, 60–62ff.). This is to say, if there is parallax, there can never be only one. And, the unresolvability of parallax will have always been a remainder of the only fundamental possibility of imagination, understanding, and hope. The maintenance of such parallax, as we are elaborating it here, the thought of the double, is precisely the responsibility of practice as thought.

What meaning does this passage through the references to Kant and Karatani have for us, or what can such mean, in the horizon of the ensemble

Example   9

of problematics crisscrossing, as some possible impossible whole, the thought of the future that I am proposing herein?

Let us turn, at this conjunction, and translate this discussion of parallax in the direction of the thought of Du Bois, leaving aside and open for future consideration—that of others as well as our own—much remainder. I take recourse first to Du Bois's signal thought of "a sense of double consciousness" that took shape within a certain formation of subjectivation—as a "Negro" and an "American," within a certain historicity, the turn to the twentieth century—and the critical capacity it allows, a kind of "second sight" in that world, namely, that "American world," in which it arose.

> After the Egyptian and Indian, the Greek and Roman, the Teuton and Mongolian the Negro is a sort of seventh son, born with a veil, and gifted with second-sight in this American world,—a world which yields him no true self-consciousness, but only lets him see himself through the revelation of the other world. It is a peculiar sensation, this double-consciousness, this sense of always looking at one's self through the eyes of others, of measuring one's soul by the tape of a world that looks on in amused contempt and pity. One ever feels his two-ness,—an American, a Negro; two souls, two thoughts, two unreconciled strivings; two warring ideals in one dark body, whose dogged strength alone keeps it from being torn asunder. The history of the American Negro is the history of this strife,—this longing to attain self-conscious manhood, for merge his double self into a better and truer self. In this merging he wishes neither of the older selves to be lost. He would not Africanize America; for America has too much to teach the world and Africa. He would not bleach his Negro soul in a flood of white Americanism, for he knows that Negro blood has a message for the world. He simply wishes to make it possible for a man to be both a Negro and an American, without being cursed and spit upon by his fellows, without having the doors of Opportunity closed roughly in his face. (Du Bois 1903d, 3–4, chap. 1 paras. 3–4)

Should we not recognize Du Bois's formulation on "the meaning of being black at the dawning of the Twentieth Century," as he put it in the "forethought" of his book of *The Souls of Black Folk* of 1903—a form of "seeing oneself through the eyes of the other world"—as addressing in its own manner the horizon of question that Kant broached in his 1766 ruminations on metaphysics (with Europe awash with the heights of the beneficence arising from a then three-centuries-old Atlantic slave trade, for example) (Du Bois 1903d, 3–4, chap. 1, paras. 3–4)? And too, should we not see within the movements of Du Bois's discourse of a "second sight"—a form of parallax, or better, a movement of "pronounced parallaxes," as Kant put it, but here shaded "darkly as through a veil"—that allowed Du Bois to open a critical thought not just on an "American world" of the turn to the last century, but rather on the whole trajectory of modern historicity, including especially its epistemic gathering, in which a critical production such as Kant's (and Marx's too) could arise, which yielded for Du Bois the theoretical intervention of his own elaboration across some six subsequent decades a discourse of a global level "problem of the color line" emerging over the half-dozen centuries before our own and remaining at stake within our moment for those yet to come (Du Bois 1903d, 3, 8, chap. 1, paras. 3 and 9; Du Bois 1900; Du Bois 2015d)?

For, indeed, it was this double and redoubled sense of critical perspective that allowed Du Bois to think otherwise than an alignment with a dominant Europe or a strident and precipitative America, and prophetically as it were with regard to Asia as a whole—to nominalize an example, which would name not only Japan and China, but India, Korea, Indonesia, the Philippines, Vietnam, and so forth—indexing in this case the massive attempts by the European powers and the United States at the complete colonization of the vast majority of the world across the second half of the nineteenth century and into the twentieth. Indeed, the reference here is to the colonial and postcolonial global level horizon as some kind of ensemblic whole. Thus, finally, it was that Du Bois proposed to name the possibility of an Asian future—which we now remark as a certain sense of an Afro-Asia to come—for example, as other than that bequeathed to the world by the "West." For was it not indeed his sense of the possibility of another world, a future different than what that "West" had made it in the past, that gave the bias, the critical edge to Du Bois's sense of world history astride the years following the First World War, and before the Second World War had fully announced itself, when so much of our contemporary sense of the world historic interest of modern Asia (now definitively remarked in its implication by its Diasporas) was quite literally being fought out on a global scale? The neutrality of a certain liberalism—a kind of Kantianism (whether self-reflexively understood by the thinkers in question or not) if you will—is not presumed within Du Bois's practice. Nor can the putative universalism

Example   11

of a certain Marxism be simply granted by his reflection. While remaining otherwise than a naive realism, according to Du Bois's practice, there is no way into and through our sense of historicity than its production of what is at stake for us here and now—even despite or otherwise than any hope we maintain about the future.[1]

For, in this path of reflection, Du Bois's itinerary of the double, or a new theoretical sense of critical parallax, the practice of thought does not arrive at a "unanimous" or common understanding of difference as a simple formation. Yet, neither is it an account of a mode of "parallelism" to or within various forms of limit within modernity, nor a contraversion or "counter" formation of the same; and less still is it a simple "duality."[2] Along with the feints and dissimulations that attend its emergence, its yield remains as both a problem and a critical resource (two ways of formulating the same matter)—of existence and thought as practice (Chandler 1993). In turn, its problematic status, that is, its partiality, is precisely the source of its generativity. It must always reference the more than one or affirm such as its futural historicity, which is already at stake in its present as given. And, in only an apparent paradox, this partiality is precisely its way of acceding to a sense of possibility (rather than simply a given whole or idea of totality), which in its reception of the heterogeneity of originary irruption is both more radical and more fundamental than the long-standing dominant avatars of freedom and universality. It is both of, but remains always an exorbitance to, all senses of limit within the given that make it possible. It will thus have always remained a radical order of name for the general possibility of the historicity in which and according to which it could be announced.

And, further, for example, by way of theoretical metaphor, Du Bois's thought of the double can be understood to announce the irruption of a certain "pronounced parallax," which reveals irreversibly, in turn, that within the very possibility of seeing there is not now, nor has there ever been, any sustainable way of claiming or maintaining a supposed prior or ultimate order of simple or pure sight. Or, that is to say, sight can arise only according to a certain distribution of shading or shadow, hue, and color.

It is here then that we can turn further still, as if by way of an axis, but in truth more as if by way of the receptive tracking of the movements of shadow on the sundial, toward the horizon as such, remarking thereby the inception of our path of reflection, the irruption of the historial under the heading named African American.

Understood according to a certain historical sense encoded in Du Bois's formulation, the African American problematic can be understood to open on its other side to a whole dimension of historicity, one perhaps susceptible to a certain inhabitation. It is that dimension that in truth can be said to open the historical form of the question of the African American. Du Bois places it under the heading of the "*problem* of the color line." A critical thought of the problem of the color line proposes the terms of an epistemic desedimentation of historicity, not only of the past, but also of the present, in such a manner that one can remark the limits of such historicity as yet also outlining the thresholds by which one could reimagine possibility. It is in this sense that a continual desedimentation of the past is of fundamental necessity in practical thought. In this sense, a certain thinking of the problem of the color line might allow a different sense of world, a different sense of horizon, to arise. It would be one that is different than what has been given in the present. This too, as I have begun to propose, is the scene of a fundamental epistemological contribution by Du Bois that has yet to be fully elaborated as a theoretical intervention in modern thought as critical discourse.

In such a world, another one, different than those which have yet existed, and specifically one in which "the problem of the color line" has been rendered obsolete, groups such as the African American, *whose originarity necessarily remains at stake in every instance of its promulgation* and thus always in a sense yet to come, might be exemplary for human existence: not exemplary as the final or absolute example, but rather, exemplary of the historicity of our time and of the possibility of the making and remaking of ideals in, or as, the matter of existence in general.

However, it must be remarked that one of the astonishing facts about the current resurgence in the reading and study of Du Bois's works is the absence of any true scholastic account of his formulation and deployment of the thought of a global "problem of the color line."[3] While it remains that his most famous words are "the problem of the twentieth century is the problem of the color line," this oft-quoted statement has been understood or used primarily for its apparently prosaic truth or as if it were merely apocryphal. Thus, the phrase has been primarily used over the decades, if taken up at all, as a slogan or idiom. It has not been taken up so much as the name of a fundamental motif in Du Bois's thought or as a problem for contemporary thought in general: one that would fundamentally be epistemological even as it is irreducibly political.

In terms of the discussion of Du Bois's discourse itself, due, perhaps, to this same limited effort to think with him on this line, it has often been deduced or implied that a global perspective arose more or less suddenly

Example 13

for him as an effect of his participation in the *Exposition Universelle* held at Paris, and the first international conference called by the name "Pan-African" in London during the months of June and July in 1900.[4] And then others have operated this logic with reference to many other dates in his later career, with some mentioning the 1920s as a time when such a perspective developed, and others proposing that such an event occurred as late as 1945, when Du Bois was in his late seventies. This kind of premise and such logic has governed much of the interpretation of Du Bois's thought with regard to modernity as a whole or as it concerns the global in general no matter what period of his itinerary has been under discussion. Yet such a premise does not bear up under scholastic scrutiny and the theorizations and interpretations deduced by way of it are profoundly misleading for any attempt to judge the implication of the itinerary of Du Bois's practice for contemporary thought. Thus, it should be understood as both a scholastic paradox and a political conundrum, certainly definitive in the American and Anglo-European academic discourse, but perhaps decisive in other geo-epistemic domains by way of the dissemination of such discussion, that most people—including many Du Bois scholars—know the famous line, "the problem of the twentieth century . . ." from the reprinting of his 1901 essay "The Freedmen's Bureau," as the second chapter of *The Souls of Black Folk*, with virtually no idea of the fundamental level of sedimentation that it has within his thought: (1) that the global perspective adumbrated in that chapter was developed initially from Du Bois's attempt to understand the specific African American situation; (2) that it bespeaks a whole conception situated at a global level that Du Bois had begun to formulate during the half-dozen years prior to the publication of his most famous book; and (3) that it remained an epistemological formulation that he would elaborate on many registers across his entire career, serving to formulate the theoretical horizon for the most ambitious works of the later stages of his career, from *Black Reconstruction* in 1935, including both *Color and Democracy* and *The World and Africa* from the signal era at the end of the Second World War, to *The Black Flame* trilogy from 1955 to 1961 (Du Bois 1976a; Du Bois 1975a; Du Bois 1976d; Du Bois 1976c; Du Bois 1976b; Du Bois 1976e).

It is for this reason that a kind of restatement of the paradoxes engendered by this mistaken approach can perhaps underscore the still timely pertinence of a clarification of the issue at hand. So, on the one hand, those who know of the line just quoted from the second chapter of *The Souls of Black Folk* usually have a quite limited sense of its global framing in Du Bois's thought; or, if they do gesture toward such a frame, they have little or no grip on the depth of the conception involved. But, on the other hand, those who rhetorically grasp this line as a way to link Du Bois's thought to a global context in a general sense, tend to do it by using it as a kind of weapon, under the authority of his name, against what they mistakenly think or opportunistically characterize as a kind of paro- chialism in the discourse of African Americans in the United States, or the apparent historic dominance of such a topic in discussions of the question of the African Diaspora or the problem of race in a global context.[5] Yet the pertinence of such announced interventions might at best be their rendering legible matters of position and authority in our contemporary discursive and institutional scene. For beyond any matter of polemics, it remains that the most troublesome aspect of readings of Du Bois that would conscript his discourse primarily for affirming our own ideas about the truth of modern global history is that it makes it very difficult if not impossible to access and to judge, first on the terms of Du Bois's own declarations, what he thought he was saying.

If one undertakes such an examination, it renders a quite legible track that shows Du Bois was first led to this global frame precisely by trying to think the African American situation in the United States in the most fundamental and general manner possible. That he was, in this sense, first solicited by the specific ground of his own emergence articulates a general protocol of a commitment to thinking immanence that one disavows at one's own epistemic peril. That he sought to situate such immanence in relation to a passage of thought to the most general itself solicits and radicalizes this thought of the specific and the immanent. In an empirical sense this meant that he was led to a global frame precisely *by way of* this preoccupa- tion with the situation of African Americans in the United States and *not despite* it. Yet, in a theoretical sense, Du Bois was *simultaneously* insisting that the African American situation could only be understood as part of a global horizon and that global modernity could only be understood if one recognized the constitutive status for the making of modern world history as a whole of the historical process by which this group was announced in history.[6] The African American situation was a global one for Du Bois. And, *in this way*, at a ground level of historicity, shall we say, it was an exemplary example of a global problematic.[7]

Let me briefly restage here a scholastic question that I believe suggests in succinct manner what is at issue. What if the apparently most local and parochial chapters of *The Souls of Black Folk*, if situated, for example, in relation to the labor of thought presented in the essay "The Present Out-

Example   15

look for the Dark Races of Mankind," dating from December 1899, can be rendered as profoundly marked by a global perspective (Du Bois 1900; Du Bois 2015d)? Yet what if it is also the case that it therefore becomes clear that the means to the development of such a perspective for Du Bois, that of a certain sense of global modernity, was through and through by way of his concern with the only apparently parochial or relatively local situation of the African American in the United States? I suggest that this double remarking can come into profound relief by such juxtaposition. Thus, it is of some import that "The Present Outlook for the Dark Races of Mankind," which was first presented in public in December 1899 as the presidential address at the third annual meeting of the American Negro Academy, bears at most an extremely limited citation in the contemporary literature and in an essential sense remains unread in our time. It remains that up to now there is no contemporary approach to Du Bois's work that has accomplished such an interpretive positioning.

Yet this essay is one of Du Bois's most important: for it is in fact the first place where he actually enunciates his most famous statement—the problem of the twentieth century is the problem of the color line—according to an achieved principle of formulation and clarified epistemological frame. This essay is certainly as important as "The Conservation of Races," an essay that has rightly spawned a small cottage industry on both sides of the Atlantic over the course of the past generation. Thus, it is only an apparent paradox that Du Bois's essays on the African American situation in the United States, from the time just after the completion of his doctoral study in 1895 to the years immediately following the publication of *The Souls of Black Folk* in 1903, and especially including the chapters of the latter text that to a superficial reading would appear most particularistic; for example, those on the "Freedmen's Bureau" or on the "relations of Black and White Americans in the South," acquire their most powerful legibility and theoretical importance, then or now, only when seen as the very path for Du Bois's development of an interpretation of modernity in general, certainly of America as a distinctive scene of its devolution, but also of a global or worldwide historical conjuncture understood from the trajectory of human history as a whole. For taken as a whole singular enunciation, even as it is threaded with multiple motivations, claims, and levels of utterance, Du Bois's discourse at the turn of the twentieth century bespeaks a powerful sense of the way that the question of the African American is a question about the possibilities of a global modernity in general. Such an understanding should play a large role in getting rid of an often understated but widely held sense that the study of African Americans in the United States is a parochial or naively nationalistic discussion, and so forth. It can also go far in showing that in fact the problem of the Negro in America has long been understood within the most astute configurations of the African American intellectual community in the United States as a fundamental part of the question of colonialism and its aftermath, that the differentiation of the two discourses, for example, one concerned with "African American" matters and another concerned with "the colonial" in general in contemporary academic discussions in the Americas and in Europe, but especially in the United States, is an instituted one of recent and superficial lineage. We can underscore, that Du Bois, for example, from the very inception of his itinerary had announced a conception of a thought of the African American in which the premise and implication of this common historicity was the very terms of enunciation.

In the context of contemporary discussions about the aftermath of colonialism, or postcolonial discourse of one kind or another, or debates about globalization, Du Bois's early negotiation of the epistemological paradoxes involved in conceptualizing the modern history of imperialism, slavery, and colonialism in a way that accounts for its worldwide provenance and does not simply reproduce a self-congratulatory narrative of the making of the West, along with his prophetic thematization of *the way in which* the question of historical difference (for which we have no good names—such as ethnicity, race, nationality, culture, etc.) among groups of people would come to dominate future discussions of politics and authority in general on a global level in the twentieth century and beyond, bear renewed and somewhat paradoxical force (Chandler 2006b; Chandler 2007). Thus, the current discussion of Du Bois must be rearticulated such that it may become possible to thoroughly think through the implications for contemporary thought of his understanding of the African American situation as part of a worldwide problematic, whether we call it modernity or postmodernity, the persistence of colonialism, or postcolonialism, a conflict of civilizations, or simply globalization or *mondialisation*, or something else altogether.

On such a path of critical thought, the African American example— by way of Du Bois's elaboration of its configuration in the movement of an always at least and never-only double organization of heading—might appear as precisely a resource in a new thought of contemporary historicity.

Second, we might say, to continue our elaboration on the track of this order of example, Du Bois was concerned with *the question of* Africa—certainly through and by way of and always in the existence of those peoples *of* the

Example   17

continent known by this name—with regard to its implication for how one might think of possibility in human history on a global scale. Such question came to him initially by way of his concern with the African American question. The two were for him inseparably interwoven. This was in the first temporal instance by way of the history of the slave trade stemming from the fifteenth century. It was also by way of the promulgation of an imperial colonialism by European states on the African continent during the latter half of the nineteenth century. Yet, it must be emphasized here, in a way that contravenes the too common formulation of question in contemporary discussions that have proceeded under the heading of the postcolonial for the past generation or so, that from within the horizon of the twenty-first century one can only get to the problem of the global level of modern colonialism by way of a first coming to terms with or passing through the history of modern systems of enslavement announced across the Atlantic and in the Americas. This earlier moment then is the incipient reference for Du Bois's theorization of Africa as a problematic of his present. The latter moment is the very time of Du Bois's first formation as a thinker, thereby naming both what is at stake for him and the practical nominal presentation of historicity that organizes the directions of the initial steps of his inquiry. However, within his engagement with these two specific references, given by time and place, Du Bois's concern with the historial character of Africa was general and fundamental. As such, it can be said that its futural status remained for him the question of the future of *the whole* of the world. His question, announced already in the 1890s at the very beginning of his itinerary and persisting throughout all stages of his work, even right to the end, was about the place of Africa in world history, that is, in the historicity of world. Three tracks might be remarked: the place of ancient Egypt in historicity, both its relation to historial groups in other parts of the continent and its relation to the history of human civilization in a general or global sense; the original character of historical practice among groups throughout the continent; and the possible futures for the new forms of historical entity that had already become definitive, or would shortly become so, especially political entities, across the African continent. The place of a "pan-African" proclamation for Du Bois then turns on the question of how to inhabit an historically given situation: that the devolution of modernity has been in its fundamental organization by way of the production of something that he called, from early on in his writings, "the Negro problems." Thus, Du Bois's abiding concern for a putative Africa was for the production of a collective subject (political or legal, economic, and ideological or "cultural") that could respond to this historic denegation, transform it, and move beyond its horizon to an alliance with the most far reaching possibilities of human freedom as such had emerged in the modern epoch.

It should be remarked here, for it has yet to be generally understood, that Du Bois's concern with Africa is the place of a major intervention (like so much else in his itinerary): the resolute proposition of the principle of elucidating and interpreting the historical form or organization of groups on the African continent as an indication of an original historicity as such. This is the root narrative movement of this 1915 text, *The Negro* (Du Bois 1975d). I consider it in an epistemic sense the pioneering statement of a possible African studies in the discourses of the United States and for discourses that would try to think the Continent and its Diaspora together, even if it was not programmatic in register and even if today it still remains unrecognized as such in general.[8] It is perhaps this "pan-Africanism" that later academic Africanist discourse thought it should disavow in the name of a supposedly more impartial perspective. The epistemic bearing of Du Bois's attempt remains as pertinent today as it was in 1915. This bearing is organized along two inextricably interwoven lines of implication: first, that the specific forms of inhabitation and practice by groups of sub-Saharan Africa are of basic implication for the interpretation of the meaning of human practice in the *modern* era in general; second, that given its distinct role in the making of the modern world systems of power—political and economic—in which its exploitation could be proposed as an irreducibly decisive and historically determining means of the passage to the modern in the West, its *historically* given status stands as a judgment of the same and an arbiter of futural limit for the world in general. The great surge in the excavation and elaboration of the symbolic that has been definitive in the study of the continent since the 1960s, building on premises that were institutionalized in the 1930s and 1940s in the United States, was already proposed by Du Bois in his early text. And while Du Bois had already disavowed any biological determinism to the concept of race in his 1897 text "The Conservation of Races," in the 1915 text he explicitly declared the impertinence of such putative determination for conceptualizing something called "the Negro" in a global sense as well as for thinking the relation of Africa and "its" historic Diaspora. The thought of a "black Atlantic" or a horizon of "Africana" as an epistemic problematization is already assayed in his discourse at the advent of the First World War. As such, Du Bois had broached the very question that would be another key term in the formulation of both an academic African studies and an academic African Diasporic

Example   19

studies from the 1930s forward and has since remained a perennial—even if at times submerged—nexus of question.

With all of this in mind we can excerpt a passage from Du Bois's concluding words in his 1915 text, his first sustained discussion of Africa, and take note of that poignant irony that is the very lacing by which so much of his writing is sustained. It points us toward a radical thought by which the name of "Africa" stands not as an indication of a closed and primordial figure in the history of the modern world, whether such might be understood as a good thing (the Africa of a reactionary pan-Africanism) or bad thing (the Africa of an unjustifiably presumptive European philosophy), but as the scene by which the passage of historial possibility might be tracked and perhaps announced.

> There is slowly arising not only a curiously, strong brotherhood of Negro blood throughout the world, but the common cause of the darker races against the intolerable assumptions and insults of Europeans has already found expression. Most men in this world are colored. A belief in humanity means a belief in colored men. The future world will, in all reasonable probability, be what colored men make it. (Du Bois 1975d, 146)

This apparently prosaic proposition by Du Bois mobilizes an ensemble of highly overdetermined terms in the first sentence of its statement, appearing in one register of its enunciation to thereby reaffirm them. Nonetheless, it can be understood to produce an ironic displacement of their pertinence. For the second, third, and fourth sentences of the passage take up the apparent nominal limit as it is announced in the terms of the historical present—the figure of the "colored"—and affirms it as the name of a possibility that would extend in every sense—spatial and temporal—beyond such limit. Thus, his reinscription of the terms of historical limit as they were announced in his historical present sustains an ironic affirmation which would precisely mark as relative such limits and point toward an exorbitance within that very historicity. The name of Africa, then, may well be understood therein to remain as the paleonymic inscription for such possibility beyond the limit of world.

Third, in a manner that we have already begun to remark by way of reference to the African American example in the United States and the question of the African example, Du Bois was concerned with a global horizon to which he would give many names across his long life (some that we might affirm today and others that we would most likely reject), such as "the dark races of mankind" in 1900 or "worlds of color" in 1925 and again in 1961 or the "dark colonized laborers of the world" in 1944. Elucidating this horizon, characterizing its historicity, and effecting a transformation of the conditions of its emergence and persistence—the general form of modern colonialism and its aftermath—might well be taken as the most general political frame of Du Bois's life work. *The paramount question is: what might these massed millions, now billions, contribute to the making of possibilities for the future of human existence in a global sense if they were free to cultivate their most specific and originary character to its fullest.* (And such character would have no determination that could be understood simply on the basis of an a priori, such as the biological premise of the concept of race.) It appears as an achieved epistemological focus as early as December 1899, on the occasion of his first presentation of the text, "The Present Outlook for the Dark Races of Mankind," in the form of a public lecture (Du Bois 1900). It can then be tracked across his entire career and registered at every level of his discourse: for example, in summary restatement as a declaration in "The Color Line Belts the World" (1906) (Du Bois 1906a); as the global frame that is especially resounded in the last two chapters of *John Brown* (1909) (Du Bois 1973a) and which later resonates as the drone throughout that complicated evening *raga* that is *Black Reconstruction* (1935) (Du Bois 1976a); as the guiding interpretive principle of "The African Roots of War" (1915) (Du Bois 1915; Du Bois 1982a), as well as *Darkwater* (1920) (Du Bois 1975b) and "Worlds of Color" (1925) (Du Bois 1982f); as the operative question at stake in the narrative of *Dark Princess* (1928) (Du Bois 1974a); as the governing thought in the unpublished epistolary narrative "A World Search for Democracy" (1937) (Du Bois 1980d), and in the epistemological coda for it that is *Color and Democracy* (1945) (Du Bois 1975a); and as the telic problematic of the *Black Flame Trilogy* (1957–1961), especially its last volume *Worlds of Color* (1961) (Du Bois 1976c; Du Bois 1976b; Du Bois 1976e). This is the track of a whole possible investigation into the thought and contributions of Du Bois at a level of profundity that has not yet been attempted. This order of attention would mean that both the object, the "thought of Du Bois," and the required subject of inquiry would doubtless exceed the terms of a discourse signed by one author or encoded in one textual statement. It should be the operative horizon by which Du Bois's thought is reengaged critically and articulated as a an essential reference within the scene of a most contemporary and ongoing global-level discussion.

Example 21

Most profoundly here a certain form of hyperbolic renarrativization of the world historical would be the most fundamental demand. Is this not the practice of that mischievously erudite novel of the Harlem Renaissance—*Dark Princess*—to take but one example? World history is announced therein on the subterranean orders of existence as they have been canonically given in the figure of the West as the devolution of modern history. Thus, in the narratives of this text, the historicity of the present becomes nameable according to an ensemble of axes and temporalities that are not according to either the line or the point. In one sense, they displace topical orientation— underground there is no absolutely given direction as such. In another, they extend and interweave relation according to temporal rhythms that recognize the present only under the heading of its possible dissolution—something like the always multiple movement of the waves of the ocean. Such are the implication of the scenes of renarrativization set afoot in this novel: the interlocutions among "the council of the darker races of mankind" in its opening scenes; the "back rooms"—whether of the bar or the train—that provide the scenes for the development of an insurrectionary movement of the Negro American; in the meditations that occur in the mind's eye of our would-be hero as he serves in the excavation of an underground railroad that will go nowhere; or, in the configured imagination of the two mothers who yield the figure of a narratable history of a global south coming by way of a joining of a certain North American "south" across the "southernmost" landforms of the Americas and of Africa, and across the Atlantic and Indian oceans, to "South" Asia and thence to Asia and beyond to the "islands of the [other] sea." Such narration has to announce the possible production of the very epistemic horizon that it would proclaim as the terms of its authorization: this is a performative historiography that would extend itself beyond the temporalities and the spaces of the given understanding of historial possibility. Such is the burden and the task of the historiographic voice proposed in this narrative. It is perhaps no wonder that its demands remain at stake in our own time of interlocution.[9]

Fourth, it may surprise many to imagine Du Bois, the Pan-Africanist, as a profound thinker of the question of the historicity of Europe. Yet, it is not too much to propose that he is perhaps the most unread or underread of the major thinkers of the twentieth century on the historial figure of Europe.[10] For Du Bois, as is well enough known, Europe was reflexively at issue at the autobiographical level already from the early 1890s. What has yet to be rendered clearly is that Europe is announced as a philosophical problematic in his thought from the late 1890s onward: such is evident in two lectures that remained unpublished during his lifetime, "The Art and Art Galleries of Modern Europe" (ca. 1896) (Du Bois 1985a) and "The Spirit of Modern Europe" (ca. 1900) (Du Bois 1985b), as well as its articulation as a problem and example in "The Present Outlook for the Dark Races of Mankind" (1899), one of his most important essays, as I have already remarked and will annotate further below (Du Bois 1900; Du Bois 2015d). From this time through to the end of his career, this order of interrogation and reflection about Europe forms a fundamental line of sedimentation in Du Bois's thought, especially just before, during, and after, the First World War (Du Bois 1910; Du Bois 1915; Du Bois 1917; Du Bois 1975b). Starting from the historically given role of Europe in modern world history, the question of its historial status appears in every major aspect of Du Bois's attempts to think through the historicity of modernity. Certainly this is true everywhere that he discusses colonialism and the question of "the darker world" in the future; thus each of the texts mentioned above on this theme are pertinent here. Yet what is not so readily recognized is how in each of his major engagements with Africa, there is an abiding examination and critique of Europe; this is due to the deep mutually constituting relation, as Du Bois understands it, of these two historical entities as each are announced in modern history. Thus it is that the first three chapters of *The World and Africa* (1947), for example, are an acute questioning of the tenability of the legacies of Europe for the future as they stand just after the Second World War and at the midpoint of the century in which the global problem was "the relation of the darker to the lighter races of men" (Du Bois 1976d). And, for example, Du Bois's last major published extended narrative, the last volume of the *Black Flame* trilogy, *Worlds of Color* maintains this line as a major passage. The novel opens with the protagonist embarking on a worldwide tour, much as Du Bois had done in 1936, to inquire about the future of democracy in the world as a whole. The first stop is Europe where a sustained and ironic discussion recurs across the national historical figures of Western Europe about their respective places, as well as that of the "continent" as a whole, in such a future. In the background always is the question of how to situate Europe's past and present exploitation of the continent of Africa in world historical terms. Another superb example of this approach in Du Bois's thought is one of his last published texts, "Africa and the French Revolution," dating from July 1961.[11] What must be underscored here is the transformation in his thought about the status of Europe with regard to the terms of historicization. If at 1900 he was hopeful that Europe might still

Example   23

lead the way to a new horizon of human freedom, then an understanding of the rhythm of its unfolding was *the* essential reference for the future. And then at 1920, after the First World War, he was shocked and aghast but still hopeful about Europe; thus, a certain dialogue or appeal to Europe to affirm its original possibility as rooted in a global historical movement and to thus also affirm a recognition of historial possibility among the "dark races" of the world, remained fundamental. However, by the end of the Second World War, as he saw it, given the deep reaction still determining Europe's sense of its place in a world historical context, Du Bois felt that it was necessary to understand the historial status of this figure according to fundamentally different premises. His historiographical syntax now proposed a fundamentally different rhythm of concatenation. One can recognize such by the fact that in 1945 the proposition of a certain renarrativization of the internal historicity of Europe, although already announced in his work as early as the 1890s and persisting as a central subterranean fault or ore line throughout his career, now emerged into a distinctive concatenation and order of relief and the problem of addressing its implication took on a profoundly urgent status. Without having given up on an affirmation of the best possibilities bequeathed by Europe to global civilization, the world, as such, whatever that might be, Du Bois came to propose, by the late 1950s, ought to look elsewhere than Europe for a historial example in the decades and perhaps centuries to come. A principal reason was Europe's continuing affirmation of the premises of a putative global "color line," even if at times such persistence occurred underneath all manner of explicit disavowals.

An instructive question for the history of thought can thus be posed as the joining of the autobiographical and the historiographical: what if a certain "Europe" to come might imagine that one W. E. B. Du Bois—Negro, African, Afro-Caribbean, African American, Black, American, European American, White, European, and so on—is one of its most distinguished practitioners of thought from the nineteenth and twentieth centuries? If so, then might not his demand for a rethinking of its horizon lend itself to a certain radicalization of its historial possibility? Might not then the indefatigable commitment to thinking beyond the limit of world that is registered at the most radical levels of his discourse be an exemplary example for the proposition of such possibility? It is in this sense that one can wonder if what has been proposed as a question for Europe at the inception of the current century, may yet be recognized as already formulated and in these profound terms under the heading of "the *problem* of the color-line" at the inception of the last one (Du Bois 1900; Du Bois 2015d)?

Who counts, can be given an account, or can be given, as European? Who, or what, then, (is) Europe?

Finally, in this adumbration, it must be said that for Du Bois, Asia was not simply one example among others. The most important aspect of this historical domain for Du Bois was that its major bearing for world history in the modern epoch—in the planetary sense—remained *yet to come*. Let us note first that its boundaries for him were not fixed. It would include, certainly, what would have been called the "Far East," from the standpoint of America, such as Japan, China, Korea, and Southeast Asia (Taiwan, the Philippines, Indonesia, etc.); but also in his variegated discussions of "Russia," the latter remains ambiguously at the limit of both East and West, both geographically and as an historical entity (and one has the sense that he hoped it would in the future affirm its relation to a new Asia as definitive of its sense of possibility). And what he called "India" was a fundamental part of this historial profile and for him the definitive source of the great ancient codification of the thought of *generosity* in naming the possibility of a human habitation of spirit, a root that he maintained could still play a fundamental and decisive role in a world transformation of values (a sense that is most spectacularly displayed in *Dark Princess* (Du Bois 1974a), his aforementioned 1928 utopian novel, and in his deep affirmation of two major figures of twentieth-century India, Rabindranath Tagore and Mahatma Gandhi [and one notes that Du Bois called for an African American Gandhi during the 1940s more than a decade before Martin Luther King Jr. appeared on the scene]). And then, the countries of "Eastern" Europe were also potentially part of this domain, especially Romania and Turkey, along with the Baltic states (perhaps paradoxically for some), on the one hand, and the historic peoples of Central Asia, on the other. (In his posthumous *Autobiography*, he included a separate chapter on countries of this region—marking them out as somewhat distinct from a putative Europe—wherein, he put them in the "pawned peoples" [Du Bois 1968, 22–28].) For Du Bois, at the present of his life course, shall we say, the region as a whole had yet to offer the definitive modern form of its answer to the complex question of the relation of its past to its future in the reorganization of its historicity that was fundamentally afoot from the nineteenth century forward. For him, "Asia's" situation made it not impossible that it could propose a path through the twentieth century and beyond—especially on the track of "the relation of the lighter to the dark races of men in Asia, and Africa, and the islands of the sea"—that would be other, perhaps, than that which has been practiced by Europe (and America would be included in this

Example   25

nominalization here) since the early centuries of the modern epoch. It was along this track that Du Bois early on, already before the turn of the century, announced a profound affirmation of the historial possibility that he thought Japan might propose as it at appeared at the edge of the twentieth century independent of European or American imperial colonial authority. It was an affirmation that he would never relinquish, even over the course of and in the aftermath of the tragedies of Japanese imperialism in Asia, for example, its colonization of Korea and parts of China, notably Manchuria, along with its ongoing colonial subsumption of the Ryūkyū islands (now known as Okinawa in general), and the massacre at Nanking in China in 1937 just after his first visit to the region in late 1936, and through the deep contradictions that its fascist alliance with Hitler and Mussolini in the Second World War posed for his hope. And, then *from a similar disposition,* after the inception of the revolution in China, following the Second World War, his unhopeful hopefulness for this country during the first quarter of the twentieth century found a source of renewal and transformation, and he affirmed what he imagined from that time through to the end of his life was the form of the proposition of an alternative path to true democracy. Across the maintenance of his affirmation for these two "colossi" of Asia (that is, China and Japan) as he had called them in the early 1930s, what bears sustained meditation is a certain paradoxical reciprocity of premise and hope in his understanding of Asia as a certain whole—that is as the name of a problem: (1) that "progress" in the liberation of humankind entails a "cost," including the mistakes of leadership, and that from such a position, for him, the Western nations and states of his present had no basis to censure, to pass judgment on, those of the East in their failures and limits, given the former's own imperial past and present, unless they were to renounce hope in their own commitment to the eventual realization of fundamental democracy; while (2) these two countries, Japan and China, along with other countries of the region whose profile on a regional and global level astride the twentieth century might appear smaller in the political sense (but a situation that did not necessarily translate, for him, as suggesting that they were less rich in the implication of their internal historicity on a global level), had the capacity if pursued by way of *genuine democratically derived internal* leadership to offer a future world something other than what had yet been seen, especially in the modern epoch dominated in its latest centuries by the rise of the modern imperialism of Europe and America. In principle, it can be said, Du Bois felt no apology for the historical limits of these two historial figures, whose possibilities he had affirmed. For, it might be said that what is at stake in their present remains not so much or simply in the form of the future as an ideal yet to be properly glimpsed but the immanent struggle with historicity as it is announced in existence. Du Bois continued to hope that Japan and China, for example, and Asia in general, would develop a genuinely democratic internal organization of economy and resource such that it would forego the imperial imperative endemic to all past forms of a global level organization of relation in the modern context. Thus, in their realization of the possibilities of fundamental internal democracy they might affirm a new sense of what such could actually become beyond the examples that had as yet been offered in the West.

A persisting paradox of Du Bois's thought of global imperialism must be underscored here. It is a conundrum within his itinerary of which we can be justly critical on the basis of premises that we can recognize within the fundament of Du Bois's own discourse and practice in thought. We can enter the discussion on the terms of Du Bois's affirmation of the outcome of the Japanese-Russian war of 1904–1905. (And, we should note that he followed its progress far more closely than he did the 1904–1905 Russian Revolution, a fact that he would obliquely qualify throughout the remainder of his itinerary.) Yet the matter is distinctly revelatory of the relation between the legible political order of possibility and its epistemic dimensions. (1) While Du Bois was well aware that both Russia and Japan were seeking to establish an imperial domination over Korea in this instance, in a manner that he would retain, he consistently overlooked the full destructive character of Japan's imperial ambition and practice in order to affirm the possibility that it might eventually serve as a limitation for the imperial projects of Europe, especially Great Britain, and the United States, in Asia. Thus, Du Bois's desire, we might say, to mark a limit to European and Euro-American imperial domination at the turn of the twentieth century is one of the complicated sources of his ambivalent gestures in this domain. From the temporal standpoint of the opening years of the twenty-first century, the unwritten thematic history of both when and how from one turn of the century to the next the national profile of Japan took on the characteristic features of a certain "whiteness" or "Europeanness," not to say a certain "Americanness," in the context of a global scenography, is of considerable bearing here, notwithstanding that it should remain in question and at stake just what any of such so-called proper names might mean. (2) In addition, on a broader plane, the epistemic, Du Bois understood historical change as entailing "cost." And often, according to each level of historical analysis, the question as to whether such change might be understood as "progress"

Example 27

or an ultimate good would remain open or susceptible to only an ambivalent answer for him. Quite obviously, for those who are familiar with his discourse, this did not mean that Du Bois was incapable of distinct and decisive historical judgment. On the contrary, for the conundrum persists on another level of generality. A handful of examples can be adduced here. It is the sort of question with which he closes the poignant essay "Of the Meaning of Progress," in *The Souls of Black Folk: Essays and Sketches* of 1903 (Du Bois 1903a). It is likewise for the closing two chapters of his biography *John Brown* of 1909 (Du Bois 1973a). Or, one finds it as a leitmotif running through the novel *Dark Princess: A Romance* from 1928 (Du Bois 1974a). And, it can be remarked, as a counterpoint to a temporal focus on the turn of the century, that such a question remains as an undergirding interrogation in the essay *Color and Democracy: Colonies and Peace* from 1945 (Du Bois 1975a), serving as a limit question for testing the arguments of those from Europe and America that would maintain the benevolence of colonial protectorates and a European and American domination of institutions of global governance following the Second World War. Then, in *The Black Flame* trilogy (written during the first half of the 1950s, but published across the last years of the decade), especially in its final installment, *Worlds of Color* (Du Bois 1976e; Du Bois 1957–61), this horizon of judgment can be shown to serve as the very palimpsest on which the narrative unfolds. (3) And, finally, this paradox in Du Bois's thought is rooted in the historial soil of a much larger problematic, one that extends far beyond his discourse, to which the essay "The Present Outlook for the Dark Races of Mankind" from the turn of the century already pointed: namely, the complicated relation between concepts and histories of "race" and "nation" in the different parts of the world, one involving the history of science and philosophy in Europe and America in its relation to practices of distinction or institutions organized by something called race, on the one hand, and a history informed by the complicated historial profiles of China and India across the differential formations of identity in the Indian Ocean or Pacific regions, especially in religion, whether linked to a state or not, along with a powerful discourse of "national" singularity in Japan, on the other. At stake in each of the latter instances would be the question of the singularity or justification of those who would claim the authority to rule. And, then the extent to which the discourse of science has played its own role in the promulgation of a discourse of race and might overlay, displace, or recuperate such antecedent presumptions since the eighteenth century remains a crucial horizon for research: one that is primarily yet to acquire its full profile. That these paradoxes arise from a dimension of historicity that cannot be addressed on the order of a decision, a supposedly proper judgment, is what yields the instability of Du Bois's own locutions in this domain. He would simultaneously avow the openness of history and yet seek to realize a decisive intervention within it. Japan, then, should be understood in Du Bois's discourse as an early name of this conundrum. China, later, would become another. (And, it remains that for Du Bois, Russia in its eventuality took its place here and not in a narrative of the figure of Western Europe.) And, India remained perhaps his most romantic dream on the terrain of this problematic. Asia—if there is such—thus, placed at stake the most difficult dimensions of Du Bois's thought of the status of sovereignty in our time.

A special notation should perhaps be offered here, as we engage Du Bois's thought anew. In the most radical sense, the name Asia as an epistemic entity and a concern of theoretical understanding for Du Bois should not be understood to indicate a figure that would appear as representing the side of a putative "color line," for such could be understood to hypostasize the existence of both the line and the figure as if either were a primordial entity. And then, even if one assumed for Du Bois the ontological given-ness of such a distinction, he would have positioned Asia in general with African Americans and the "darker races" of the world in relation to such a putative line. Instead, the name of Asia should be understood as proposing for him a possible example of a way to announce a form of historial order that would transpose, displace, and render practically incoherent, a historical situation or problematic—the global *"problem* of the color line."[12] This would be the proposition that is sustained in both Du Bois's practical political affirmation of Japan, China, India, and Asia, in general, throughout the twentieth century and the utopian thought of the exemplary dissolution of the problem of the color line in the narrative of *Dark Princess* from 1928 and the trilogy of *The Black Flame* from 1957 to 1961, for example. Asia is then that other name for futural possibility "beyond this narrow Now" (Du Bois 1903d, 213, chap. 11, para. 13) and beyond the limit *of* world.

Exemplarity

It is perhaps with this sense of the ontological and epistemological hospitality that defined the thought of Du Bois that the ontological order of attention to the historial therein can now be understood as also fundamentally practical—pragmatic in a general sense of the term (and I do not mean to associate him with what is generally understood as philosophical pragmatism). That is to say that his affirmation of the differential articulation of historial profile in a global scenography was neither monumentalist nor antiquarian, nor rooted in a premise of universal sympathy that would be oriented by the terms of loss or redemption, nor guided by the idea of ultimate perfectibility, for example, such as that given in an ostensibly secular and putative "cosmopolitanism" as that idea has taken shape in the supposed "West," or such as that given in the figuration of the divine throughout the world, for example the so-called East. Although it remains that he would reject none of these "ideals" as a source of possibility. Rather, Du Bois's affirmation was a pragmatic problematization of the past such that its organization could be shown to yield the very terms for the formulation of hope for a future that had not yet shown its face or found its right of historial passage. And the sense of pragmatic here is general, referring to the practicality of a task that must be or will be addressed by our action—even our supposed nonaction—no matter our disposition.

Such affirmation of the human was not grounded in a naive anthropologism. It was rather recognition of the bearing of something exorbitant to the human within the devolution of human practice. Such a thought appears at the surface of Du Bois's textual discourse by way of the abstract terms, *freedom* or *chance*. However, equally, it appears according to the shape of historical problem in the form of historial exemplar. At stake in each instance of such appearance is a question that might be given a generalized form as follows: *what is the status of relation and historical possibility?* Will the organization of relation on a global scale enhance or proscribe the disseminal realization of originary possibility?

The terms that Du Bois adduced to begin to address the question of a global-level order of historicity at the turn of the twentieth century should thus be recalled here on its own general epistemic terms. As I have already suggested, above in my discussion of the African American example, Du Bois's thought of the global horizon of modern historicity under the heading of "the problem of the color line" must be rearticulated such that its theoretical implication for contemporary thought of the colonial and postcolonial can most usefully recognized. While the phrase "the problem of the twentieth century is the problem of the color line" by Du Bois is his most famous, much more well-known than "double-consciousness" or "the veil," it remains that even today, over a century after he first made this statement in December 1899, many scholars do not really know so clearly just what he meant by it (Du Bois 1900, 95, para. 3; 104, para. 19; Du Bois 2015d).

Yet, as I have already begun to suggest, it may be of great value for contemporary scholars to have a strong sense of the global level conception of history behind Du Bois's formulation of "the problem of the color line," with its emphasis on the sense of historical problem, and thus to reckon more precisely with what it might mean for critical thought and practice that would announce itself on global or planetary horizons—we might even say a certain kind of "Black studies"—in the world today and over the course of the coming decades and perhaps centuries.

While in another context I offer a rather fulsome engagement with this fundamental dimension of Du Bois's thought, here, allow me to propose a rather brief orientation to its order of questions (Chandler 2021).

At its core, the "problem" in this formulation refers to the promulgation of *categorical* forms of proscription, no matter the guise or terms under which such is carried out (the religious, the economic, the "racial," terms of "sex," sexual difference, gender, nationality, citizenship, etc.). And such proscription would entail something other and more than apparitional modes of exclusion. In fact, it names the mode of constitution of the social and historical forms of order that are at stake in general. Yet, too, the term *color* bespeaks not only problem but also possibility—the prospect of new forms and ways for groups of humans to attain or create full realization of historical capacity, or even to open the paths toward the possibility of a horizon of unlimited generation and generosity. Underneath its form(s) questions of originary irruption—the most fundamental terms of possibility—are in radical question.

The two axial orientations of Du Bois's conception are important for us. It has always been becoming global, shall we say, pertaining to the whole of the earth world (excluding no geographical region or political domain). It is historical, referring back to the inception of modernity more than half a millennium prior to the advent of the twentieth century and referring forward to the centuries to come beyond the dawning of "the third millennium of Jesus Christ" to the time of "a brown and yellow world out of whose advancing civilization the color line has faded as mists before the sun" (Du Bois 1900, 103, para. 18; Du Bois 2015d).

Yet, this conception was not a negation of Du Bois's understanding of the situation of the United States, or the Negro American therein. Rather, as suggested above, it can be confirmed by a careful reading of *The Souls of Black Folk* of 1903 that it was by way an effort to place the American context in the most broad and fundamental historical and philosophical horizon that he was led to his initial formulation of the "problem of the color line." Thus, one can find it simultaneously articulated as the broadest theoretical horizon for the announcement of the problem of his most famous text and yet also situated at its interpretive heart. Formulated on the obverse bias, this text was focused on the historicity of the African American from Reconstruction to the turn of the century and yet oriented toward producing a conception of history that could perhaps be commensurate with the century that was to come (Du Bois 1903d).

In the context of our contemporary reflections on literature one may note that this conception is equally behind all of his novels: *The Quest of the Silver Fleece* of 1911, centered on a young Black woman who leads a local revolution among sharecroppers and immigrant workers in the deep South; *Dark Princess* of 1928, centered on a South Asian "princess" and heir apparent to the throne of a regional "kingdom," who becomes the leader of an international revolutionary organization among "the dark races of mankind"; and the *Black Flame* trilogy of the mid-1950s which, although an epic of an American family from Reconstruction to the Second World War, takes its most decisive turn in the closing volume *Worlds of Color* (pub. 1961), in which the unlikely hero, a Negro American college president, takes an around-the-world trip "in search of democracy," traveling across Europe and Russia, and including visits to China and Japan (just as Du Bois had in fact done during the second half of 1936) (Du Bois 1974b; Du Bois 1974a; Du Bois 1976b; Du Bois 1976c; Du Bois 1976e).

It is the theoretical sense that runs through all of his major historical studies and texts of social analysis. This includes, for example, not only both his dissertation (published in 1896) on efforts to end the slave trade to the United States and his first independent study, *The Philadelphia Negro* of 1899, but especially his biography of *John Brown* in 1909, *Darkwater* from 1920, his magnum opus *Black Reconstruction* of 1935, *Color and Democracy* published in 1945, and *The World and Africa* as first issued in 1947. As perhaps goes without saying, it subtends all of his major autobiographical writing (Du Bois & Eaton 1973; Du Bois 1973a; Du Bois 1975b; Du Bois 1976a; Du Bois 1975a; Du Bois 1976d; Du Bois 1975e; Du Bois 1975c; Du Bois 1968).

While almost any of Du Bois's texts could offer a rich vantage point from which to recognize the place of "the problem of the color line" in his thought and practice, a reference to "The Present Outlook for the Dark Races of Mankind" from 1899, the text in which Du Bois manages to first propose those words as an independently conceived theoretical statement, provides a distinctly valuable orientation for following it across the remainder of his itinerary. As the reading of this text in contemporary discourse remains so limited, perhaps an additional value of this brief annotation is that it might encourage others to engage this text and central line of Du Bois's thinking anew with renewed critical address.

In addition, a text that Du Bois issued following the Second World War and concerned with the promulgation of the postwar order—*Color and Democracy: Colonies and Peace* from 1945—will allow an index of this problematic of "the problem of the color line" with reference to the new global order then being established, which we can situate here under the heading of the so-called Bretton Woods institutions—the United Nations, the organization that eventually became the International Monetary Fund, and so forth—whose historical horizon of operability is now in our own time undergoing a profound transformation. Hence, I will try to recognize its place within Du Bois's thought, noting specifically its reference back from the midpoint of the century to the advent of the First World War and even beyond to the very turn to the twentieth century.

Let us, then, begin by reckoning with Du Bois's own account of his thought at the turn to the new century.

Offering the presidential address to the assembled members of the then recently established American Negro Academy in the annual meeting on December 27 in Washington, DC, Du Bois opened his discourse by outlining a distinctive spatial and temporal horizon, stating to his audience that he wished to consider with you the problem of the color line not simply as a national and personal question but rather in its larger world aspect in time and space. I freely acknowledge that in the red heat of a burning social problem like this, when each one of us feels the bitter sting of proscription, it is a difficult thing to place one's self at that larger point of view and ask with the cold eye of the historian and social philosopher: What part is the color line destined to play in the twentieth century? (Du Bois 1900, 95, para. 1; Du Bois 2015d)

From that vantage point, Du Bois immediately turned to precisely declare his thesis.

It is but natural for us to consider that our race question is a purely national and local affair, confined to nine millions Americans and settled when their rights and opportunities are assured, and yet a glance over the world at the dawn of the new century will convince us that this is but the beginning of the problem—that the color line belts the world and that the social problem of the twentieth century is to be the relation of the civilized world to the dark races of mankind. (Du Bois 1900, 95, para. 2; Du Bois 2015d)

He then proceeded over the course of the thirty-two paragraphs of his discourse to outline a horizon in which the so-called Negro question in the United States is situated within an historical topography that comprises the whole of the modern era. He refers it to a past that would stretch beyond the half-millennium that precedes the advent of the twentieth century. And he indicates that for him it refers beyond the advent of the third millennium of the Christian era, our own twenty-first century. In this sense, the Negro question in the United States and the Americas more generally, are simply part of (something that we can call, following Du Bois) the problem of the centuries, the "problem of the color line."

This phrase names a heading of thought for Du Bois. The problem—as a problem of Du Bois's thought—can be stated briefly. If the so-called Negro question in the United States is not rooted in an ontological order—that is an order of human ontology usually nominated by the term *race* as it erupted in and has subsequently in part been derived from eighteenth-century natural history and classification—then what conception of history can give us the most broad and fundamental understanding of the problem, its basis, its development, and its future? How can it be changed? If the problem does not arise from some basic ontological—physical or metaphysical—difference among humans, how has it come to be? What can we learn from such a history?

To answer these questions, Du Bois operates the presumptive theoretical fiction of a putative practical whole posited as "humanity" and derives thereby the critical theoretical fiction of "the problem of the color line."[1] In the context at hand, Du Bois tries to name a theme—even if it is not a thing and does not exist, as such—that can be traced across time and space to bring into relief a submerged dimension of modern historicity on a global scale.

With regard to the past, in interpretive summary, in "The Present Outlook for the Dark Races of Mankind" Du Bois uses this critical theoretical fiction to trace practices of categorical proscription during some six centuries and more across the whole of the earth. (And I note that, by my use of the term categorical, here, I refer to claims of the possibility of a distinction that would insist on the radical possibility of a line marking or outlining a distinction of the following sort: all or nothing, either/or, only one thing counts in a given order of identification, one must be one thing and not the other, one cannot be both, and so forth.) Du Bois constructs a narrative of global space by beginning his account of the "problem" of the color line in Africa, moving through the Middle East and Asia (including a nodal stop with reference to Japan), across the Pacific Ocean, through the Americas, north and south, and then across the Atlantic, finally to include Europe, especially Western Europe. In a manner that I can only mention here, the very form of this spatial narrative, in that it rhetorically privileges the histories of the vast majority of the world—the "colored" folk of the world—carries its own thetic proposal about how one might approach a new thinking of modern global level history. Du Bois's claim is that such forms of proscription have in the past led to the downfall of civilizations, referencing the massive empires of the past millennium, annotating in different but fundamentally similar ways the historical contradictions within the Ottoman, the Mughal, the Qing, the Russian, the Portuguese, the Spanish, and the British empires, all of which were well within, or would soon enter, their death throes.

With regard to Europe in some general sense, taking it at 1900 as an example of both the problem and the possibilities for solution, Du Bois elaborates at some length the successive displacements of forms of categorical proscription across this same half millennium, that is, the contravention of proscriptions of religion, of so-called economic and social class, of political right or citizenship (including education and birth, etc.). This narrative is a history of the dissolution of absolute boundaries.

With regard to the future, the twentieth century and the centuries to come beyond it, Du Bois raised a prophetic challenge and hope. On the one hand, he hoped that "war" would diminish to such a point that any who proposed it would be ostracized. While fundamentally wrong in the instance, for we have seen the opposite on an utterly unprecedented scale in history, it expressed Du Bois's hope at that juncture that the categorical sense of friend and enemy would become difficult to sustain as a new sense of a global humanity unfolded—disrupting and dissipating the past forms of "the problem of the color line." On the other hand, Du Bois believed that a new sense of "the problem of the centuries would emerge." This new horizon—how to understand the unfolding situation in his present—was in fact his immediate and practical theoretical concern. We will see a fundamental pattern emerge, he declared to his audience in Washington, DC in December 1899.

> [A]t the same time the expansion and consolidation of nations to-day is leading to countless repetitions of that which we have in America to-day—the inclusion of nations within nations—of groups of undeveloped peoples brought in contact with advanced races under the same government, language and system of culture. The lower races will in nearly every case be dark races. German Negroes, Portuguese Negroes, Spanish Negroes, English East Indian, Russian Chinese, American Filipinos—such are the groups which following the example of the American Negroes will in the 20th century strive, not by war and rapine but by the mightier weapons of peace and culture to gain a place and a name in the civilized world. (Du Bois 1900, 107, para. 25; Du Bois 2015d)

That is to say, at 1900 above all Du Bois foresaw a future Europe, but also more generally a future global horizon, in which "nations within nations" would become the distinctive form of the "problem of the color line" in the twentieth century and perhaps beyond.

Yet, even more precisely, Du Bois was writing at the inception of a new American colonial imperialism. This he placed as the single most important development within the immediate situation of his audience of December 1899, the members of the American Negro Academy.

But most significant of all at this period is the fact that the colored population of our land is, through the new imperial policy, about to be doubled by our ownership of Porto Rico, and Havana, our protectorate of Cuba, and conquest of the Philippines. This is for us and for the nation the greatest event since the Civil War and demands attention and action on our part. What is to be our attitude toward these new lands and toward the masses of dark men and women who inhabit them? Manifestly it must be an attitude of deepest sympathy and strongest alliance. We must stand ready to guard and guide them with our vote and our earnings. Negro and Filipino, Indian and Porto Rican, Cuban and Hawaiian, all must stand united under the stars and stripes for an America that knows no color line in the freedom of its opportunities We must remember that the twentieth century will find nearly twenty millions of brown and black people under the protection of the American flag, a third of the nation, and that on the success and efficiency of the nine millions of our own number depends the ultimate destiny of Filipinos, Porto Ricans, Indians and Hawaiians, and that on us too depends in a large degree the attitude of Europe toward the teeming millions of Asia and Africa. (Du Bois 1900, 102–3, para. 17; Du Bois 2015d)

This conception, in which the matter of naming the problem at stake in the so-called Negro question in the United States led Du Bois to conceptualize a global historical and temporal horizon, in which an understanding of that question implicates the whole of modern history and the whole of modern history implicates or is encoded within that question, had already named for us a powerful example in thought and practice how the matter of—or the situation at stake for—a "Black studies" or studies of persons of "color" (or now an "ethnic" studies or "indigenous studies" too), on the one hand, so often mistakenly understood as a parochial concern, and any critical or truly profound understanding of the history of modern forms of (what we now often call) globalization, on the other, are *fundamentally implicated in and as the other in their originary formation.*

If we begin to index these formulations with some address to our own moment, perhaps its visual and sonic undertones may find resonance in the mind's eye memory of our critical reflections. As one moves, with Du Bois's axial motifs in mind, from the east according to a spatial topos that we track on the bias, we can recognize a handful of historial itineraries moving other than according to the arc of justice: Japan now hesitates and remains uncertain as it negotiates this already disaster-prone twenty-first century (both human-made and natural), amid foreboding structural difficulties of demography and industrial organization after arising through oligarchic reorganization (which remains definitive of both its economy and its politics, despite its proclamation of a democratic capitalism) in meteoric fashion as a global economic superpower across the previous half-century; China's subsequent likewise oligarchic organization and meteoric rise has posed anew questions of democracy and equality of citizenship, in what should perhaps be called the Chinas in the plural, not only for Asia but for the world (despite its proclamation of a democratic, but *now capitalist*, communism); Indonesia and India, for example, in massive epochal mobilizations of democracy and economic accomplishment, must yet still negotiate the most basic of infrastructures for their majorities in a manner that challenges all existing conceptions of polity therein; the reconfigured dynamics, respectively, of the economies of South Africa, Brazil, or South Korea, for example, must still address the fundamental difficulties for their respective futures posed by the embedded legacies of colonialism within their regional situations, not to speak of an internal dissidence within each that is still hardly within the terms of acknowledgment (including, especially, in the two former countries the ongoing dispossession of indigenous groups of their land and resource therein); and the so-called Arab world, where a whole other articulation of dreams and courage has come of age, is still yet as much tethered by the systems of international validation (economic and ideological, as well as military and political) as it has been enabled by them, and perhaps for generations yet to come; and, Europe (including and beyond the economic union) along with America, both of which must now be understood as home to the world ("nations within nations," to use the old turn of phrase, from Du Bois), where even historical difference has been rearticulated to an irreversibly transformed internal horizon, each has yet still to fully discover itself anew in this new historicity (Adelson 2005; Balibar 2004).

And yet, has this latter form of problem not now also become true even if in variegated manner of every country and every major institution (public and private) throughout the whole of the planet? And, is it not true as well that the still persistent refusal to affirm a principle of equal well-being for the whole of the human inhabitants of planet earth by the so-called democratic countries in their ongoing market driven reorganization of global governance also a persisting source of an order of conflict tending to the ultimate scale no matter its idiomatic forms—of religion, of political ideology, or economic extraction and exploitation, and the transformative resistance to such? Perhaps this was announced in the critical tendency of Du Bois thought of the centuries?

And then, is it not, most generally, in a planetary sense, that we have yet to find even a moral imagination, not to say an ethics, and certainly not a theoretical orientation, with and beyond compassion or sympathy, that would allow us—whomever "we" may be, if there is such—to carry with "the enemy" a grieving for the unlivable within life, whether as death or a form of perduring existence (Butler 2009)?

Is all this, too, not best remarked under metaphor, as another refracting form of what Du Bois named under the heading of "the problem of the color line?"

In this sense, the thought of a global *problem* of the color line, in its criticism of existing forms of limit and its proposition of new forms of possibility, if given its full radius or sounded in its full depth of resonance, as Du Bois practiced it over more than a half century, may still yet assist us in both thinking and naming our contemporary senses of horizon.

Herein, then, it might be useful to punctuate this sketch of the thought of the historiographical in Du Bois's understanding by way of a kind of folding reference—from the past to the present and the present to the past—to the two major discourses that he issued in the immediate aftermath of the Second World War: the first engaged the question of the formal mechanisms by which the global system of states in his historical present might address a future planetary horizon; the other posed its question of the futural status of human collectivity by way of one example, a certain kind of exemplar, on such horizon, that is an exemplar of an impossible possibility of a possible future, if such will have been possible. We refer to the 1945 essay *Color and Democracy: Colonies and Peace* (Du Bois 1975a) and the 1947 text *The World and Africa: An Inquiry into the Part which Africa Has Played in World History* (Du Bois 1976d).

Before we turn to offer an initial note on the question of possibility, in the latter text, under the thought of Africa and *atopia*, let us first follow in an even more preliminary manner the extensions of the critical formulations of Du Bois's thought of the problem in question by way of the former, some considerations on "color" and imperialism.

Notations on "Color" and Imperialism. On the basis of our brief references to certain fundamental aspects of his discourse, especially his early projections from the turn to the previous century, we are surely within rights to propose that Du Bois should be understood as one of the earliest and most poignant critical theorists of that century, the twentieth, not only of the promulgation of colonialism, but also of what has for some time now been called discourse concerned with the "postcolonial." If this is so, then a pivotal text in that regard is *Color and Democracy*. It will thus be our guide here as we head toward the conclusion of our brief traversal of Du Bois's thought in this historiographical domain. Yet, this text has been read all too seldom within this epistemic horizon. Here I indicate the formulation of its conceptual and theoretical address in his thought in a manner that remains all too brief.

Two access paths can be named: the theoretical incipit of the text in antecedent moments of Du Bois's discourse, dating from the earliest years of the twentieth century; and then too, its projective thesis for a future that remained to come for Du Bois (but which is a "future" that has already begun for us).

With regard to the incipit of the thought that guides Du Bois's discourse in the immediate aftermath of the Second World War, we can turn and notate that among the three or four most important essays in Du Bois's theoretical production is a brief text published in May, 1915, "The African Roots of War." This essay addressed the status of imperial rivalry in the international political and economic system as it existed in the early decades of the twentieth century (Du Bois 1915; Du Bois 1982a).

While the immediate provocation of the essay should be understood as the onset of the First World War in the summer preceding, this statement nonetheless expressed in nodal form the lineaments of an understanding of modern historicity that had already taken on a definitive shape in Du Bois's thought by the turn of the century (as expressed in signal fashion, for example, in the essay "The Present Outlook for the Dark Races of Mankind" of 1899). That thought concerned the status of "the problem of the color line" in the construction of modern global historicity in a sense that would acquire considerable density and texture as Du Bois came to elaborate it across the entire course of his subsequent itinerary. In the earliest formulations of this thought, dating from the closing years of the nineteenth century (providing, for example, a major line of thought that allowed the gathering of the essays that comprise his classic *The Souls of Black Folk: Essays and Sketches* of 1903), this problematic named the practice of forms of categorical—that is hierarchical—proscription and subsumption of social groups within a given social (political and economic) horizon, whether defined at the level of nation-states, cultures, empires, or civilizations. I recall here that the purview named in "The Present Outlook for the Dark Races of Mankind," published in 1900, stretches across the previous six centuries, comprising for Du Bois the modern epoch.

In "The African Roots of War," Du Bois brings into thematic relief what he calls there a "new Imperialism" that had taken definitive shape across the last quarter of the century just previous to the one in which he was writing, which was not just a practice of exclusion or hierarchy of one kind or another but, including and in part by way of such, also a system of direct and brutal exploitation. The conjoining of an order of exclusion that would purport to be fundamental or absolute, in its premise, to a principle of exploitation without limit (in a theoretical sense; that is, the principle of chattel slavery as an economic form) is, as such, *productive* of a whole new sense of horizon, precisely one that we might today situate as global. (Again, with reference to economic form, that is to say, cheap labor can only be understood as cheap according to a premise that would understand the domain of exploitation as beyond one's own—of self, of institution, of nation, of world. Otherwise, exploitation—like nonsustainable practices in general—are the most costly of endeavors. For, they will, in the end, bring about the terminal end, absolute ruin.) Thus, if Louis Althusser can be understood to have raised into sharper theoretical relief the epistemological intervention proposed by Karl Marx with the conception of "labor power" over and against the propositions within the discourses of traditional political economy of an historically given epistemic category of labor (labor power— or the always potential capacities of the actual or possible practical activity of those who may labor—understood in my theoretically desedimentative reading as precisely not susceptible to determinate quantification, or such determination is possible only *according to the presumptive limits of a concept of capital as the horizon for theorization*, and cannot be general or include the yet impossible possible forms of the practice of the human, and so such a determinate sense of the concept should not be understood as general, as such) then I propose that by way of Du Bois we might recognize in the path of his elaboration of a problem of the color line a thought of the critical theoretical fiction of the *colors* of labor power (Marx 1977, cf. chaps. 6 and 19; Althusser 1997, 19–24; Du Bois 1976a; Spillers 2003b, 451–57). Such a thought can be given some translative epistemological relief by way of reference to the thought of Ranajit Guha from the late 1980s, when he remarked on the conundrum that capitalism as a practice will always undercut its own theoretical orientation to universalize accumulation because it must, for its own realization, simultaneously produce in a distinctive manner domains in which the realization of wealth by way of accumulation cannot be generalized. He insisted that the colonial horizon provided the exemplary example of the production of such limit, underscoring thereby its formation as what he called "domination without hegemony." With no withdrawal from Guha's practice, moreover with an amplification of its relation to what Frantz Fanon has proposed as the constitutive place of violence within the colonial situation, I must remark that by the time of Du Bois's earliest formulations of the global "problem of the color line," the "colonial" organization of the idioms of social life (here naming the political and economic, as well as the cultural) were already everywhere general, if not consistently so, across the whole of planet earth (Guha 1997; Fanon 1961). And thus likewise such a generality should also and simultaneously be understood as susceptible to a whole other remarking that attends to the potentiality of the human as laborer as a name for possibility, beyond given forms of limit. For Du Bois, the imperial exploitation of the whole of the groups of people across the planet that took its first form in the elaboration of the system of Atlantic slavery over the two and a half centuries following the purchase on the northern coast of West Africa and their resale in Lisbon of the first historic group of thirty Africans in 1442 and which reached a certain culmination in the deliberate steady annexation of Africa across the last quarter of the nineteenth century and into the new one, marked by the stipulative agreements of the 1885 Berlin Conference, was at the root of the epochal inception of this new imperialism and the rivalry that defined its hegemonic promulgation. For, from that fateful date, we might say, for two and a half centuries, the single most distinctive form of accumulation within what is now thought of as Western Europe derived from the trade and exploitation of these rivers of "black Gold."[2]

It is thus, that Du Bois locates the deep historicity of this rivalry—incipient at the midpoint of the fifteenth century and definitive by the close of the seventeenth—as "in a real sense a prime cause" of the First World War (Du Bois 1915, 707; Du Bois 1982a, 96).[3] It should—still for us today—be understood as the historic advent of the new and modern forms of imperial accumulation. Concomitant with this rivalry, following on Atlantic slavery, this colonial exploitation of Africa as part of the high mode of European colonialism globally, made tangible the terms of a discourse in which " '[c]olor' became synonymous in the world's thought with inferiority" (Du Bois 1915, 708; Du Bois 1982a, 97). Thus, on a global level, imperial accumulation became sine qua non with the exploitation of what Du Bois would call at this time groups of persons of "color." "[T]he world began to invest in color prejudice. The 'Color Line' began to pay dividends" (Du Bois 1915, 708; Du Bois 1982a, 97).

While we can only annotate the matter here, the production of such "colors" should also be understood to indicate the inception of a horizon of possibility not only within (as a good investment) but also beyond the systems of imperial practice (as surreptitious forms of possibility always beyond contemporaneous calculation).[4]

For Du Bois, the status of this rivalry during the first quarter of the twentieth century remained distinctive. He called it "democratic despotism" (Du Bois 1915, 709; Du Bois 1982a, 98). It is this formulation that solicits our sustained attention. Beyond the mercantilism of the early modern era, with its state chartered companies as special monopolies and the high mode of colonial capital accumulation of the merchant class of the nineteenth century, respectively, "finally in the twentieth century the laborer at home [in Europe and North America] is demanding and beginning to receive part of his share" of the yield of imperial exploitation, Du Bois wrote of the time of his writing (Du Bois 1915, 709; Du Bois 1982a, 98). "It is no longer simply the merchant prince or the aristocratic monopoly, or even the employing class, that is exploiting the world: it is the nation; a new democratic nation composed of united capital and labor" (Du Bois 1915, 709; Du Bois 1982a, 98). Later on in the text of "The African Roots of War," Du Bois will specify a fundamental distinction for his thought (appearing at the denouement of the opening stage of his itinerary, just before the onset of World War I, but persisting through until the end) within the laboring classes: an "aristocracy of labor," skilled, educated, and so on, on the one hand, and the unskilled, less formally educated and so forth, on the other. It is the former group that as of the middle of the second decade of the twentieth century had been admitted "to share in the spoils of capital" (Du Bois 1915, 711; Du Bois 1982a, 101).[5]

It should be annotated here that in 1933 in his signal essays on the thought of Karl Marx and the problematic of the Negro in the United States, Du Bois would further develop this thought of a "working class aristocracy." There he wrote that they form a group between "the older proletariat and the absentee owners of capital" (Du Bois [1933] 1983, 697). The "older" form of group he also called "common labor" in this text. While referencing the African American example, he also generalizes the status of this "labor aristocracy" as "a large development of a petty bourgeoisie within the American laboring class," noting it as "a phenomenon" that postdates the discourse and itinerary of Karl Marx's own practice. Thus, in a crucial line of thought, he writes in mid-1933: "The real owners of capital are small as well as large investors—workers who have deposits in savings banks and small holdings in stocks and bonds; families buying homes and purchasing commodities on installment; as well as large and rich investors" (Du Bois [1933] 1983, 697). While individual returns might well be infinitesimal, collectively their function would always portend to the massive for the organization of capital. Writing astride the early years of the Great Depression, Du Bois proposed that the interests of this group are always bound up with the interests of capital and thus they are in principle antagonistic to the interests of "common labor" (Du Bois [1933] 1983, 697). In the earlier text, dating to almost two decades previous (and in truth it can be shown that this idea had already taken shape for him across the opening decade of the century, forming a central motif in his study of John Brown and the formal abolition of slavery in the United States, for example), Du Bois proposed that it was this reversion to an older form of hierarchy—"a reversion to aristocracy and despotism"—that "reconciled the Imperialists and captains of industry to any amount of 'Democracy'" (Du Bois 1915, 709; Du Bois 1982a, 98; Du Bois 1909; Du Bois 1973a). Likewise, we can say that his thought proposes the chiasmus: it was this reversion that reconciled "democracy" in America and Europe to imperialism and capitalist expansion through colonialism.

For theorists of the time of Du Bois's earliest writings under discussion here, this remained a confounding "paradox." On the one hand, the principle of global expansion as the path for accumulation was much theorized by the classic formulations of imperialism, from 1902 to 1916 (Hobson [1902] 1905; Hilferding [1910] 1981; Lenin [1916] 1964). Yet, on the other hand, the lineaments of Du Bois's thematization of the way in which such expansion has always and only occurred in the modern horizon as an articulating production of a "problem of the color line"—fundamentally producing a multiply refracting horizon of difference, which although occurring by way of persisting aggressive promulgations of exploitation under various categorical premises yet articulates as historical outcome only as forms of noncategorical variegation among groups of humans—remains obscured or ambivalently positioned in such work. For Du Bois's thought in his 1915 essay is not that the principle of "color prejudice" as a "dividend" within a global horizon is ancillary or simply after the fact of imperial expansion but that such principle is the very mode of the organization of such expansion across the modern period. It should perhaps be understood as the general form of capitalism as such—there is no such thing as a pure form, an unmarked generality, that can be understood as capitalism, before, prior to, or otherwise than a system constituted and organized in all its diversity and complexity as an ongoing and dynamic formation of a what Du Bois has proposed here under the heading of the "problem of the color line."

Those familiar with the magnificent text published by Du Bois in 1935 under the heading of *Black Reconstruction* will doubtless recognize that in essence I have just produced a kind of extended summary statement—by way of an account of its prehistory within Du Bois's discourse—of the theoretical intervention that guides the elaboration of its narrative of the opening, rise, and devolution of the American Civil War and its aftermath, known as the Reconstruction era. It is thus only according to this theoretical sense that the lines that open Du Bois's 1901 essay on the Freedmen's Bureau (and later placed as the head of the second chapter of *The Souls of Black Folk*) should be understood: "The problem of the twentieth century is the problem of the color line; the relation of the darker to the lighter races of men in Asia and Africa, in America and the islands of the sea" (Du Bois 1903d: 13, chapter 2, para. 1; Du Bois 1901). For with this account in mind, we can gather a rather fulsome sense of the theoretical import of the sentence that immediately follows upon that opening declaration: "It was a phase of this problem that caused the Civil War; and however much they who marched south and north in 1861 may have fixed on the technical points of union and local autonomy as a shibboleth, all nevertheless knew, as we know, that the question of Negro slavery was the deeper cause of the conflict" (Du Bois 1903d: 13–14, chapter 2, para. 1; Du Bois 1901). Slavery in the Americas, North, South. and Central, and across the Caribbean, are in and of themselves simply a nodal articulation of this global-level order of historicity that Du Bois has gathered into reflective and critical regard by way of the theoretical formulation of a "problem of the color line." While one might elaborate at some length, on the order of its detail, the specificity and general implication of the interventions and contributions proposed by Du Bois in this great text, I must leave such an elaboration proper for its own context and here propose what I have said thus far as simply a kind of introduction to the massive discourse of that text and as an overture toward the renewed engagement of it in our century, on the occasion of the sesquicentennial of the proclamations of the legal abolition of slavery in the United States and the semicentennial of Du Bois's own passage beyond.

Following the lead of Du Bois, in part, almost two generations past, Cedric Robinson proposed an analogous thought, which remains exemplary

(Robinson [1983] 2000b). In our contemporary moment Denise Ferreira da Silva can be understood to have extended and proposed a radicalization in this domain of theoretical problem, in a certain way, that is with acute regard for the whole itinerary of modern thought as announcing both the productivity and the limits of power as knowledge (Silva 2007).[6] Yet, the matter is both more profound and more simple still. For there is no given horizon of thought or critical practice that is, or can be rendered, in its contemporary formation commensurate with the problematic that may be named under the heading of a critical global history of what I propose to adumbrate as the "*colors*" of labor power—if the later may be posed as a certain form of critical theoretical fiction—in which the presumptive fiction of an unmarked form of "labor power" (the abstract potentiality of a laborer to labor) allows us to propose the critical thought of "colors" that is put into deployment here.[7]

Yet, along another trajectory of contemporary discourse, in the closing text of their trilogy proposing the new thought-metaphors of "empire," "the multitude," and "commonwealth," Michael Hardt and Antonio Negri seem hesitant at best to engage the root level dimension of this form of problem as we have begun to outline its formulation in the discourse of Du Bois, despite, on the one hand, a previous sober and lucid hesitation by a notable affirmative critic of their work on this *topos*, and their own remark (following others) of the reappearance of "old elements" of "formal subsumption" in a new "accumulation by dispossession" (here, specifically in the context of Africa) in the twenty-first century, on the other (Hardt & Negri 2000; Hardt & Negri 2004; Hardt & Negri 2009, cf. 203–48, esp. 231; Arrighi 2002, 23; Harvey 2006, cf. 69–117). (And, here, specifically in the context of Africa, the signal work of James Ferguson on this *topos* must be noted [Ferguson 2006].) That is to say, in the discourse of these coauthors they offer no noticeable account within their theoretical disposition of the motivation for the supposed "reappearance" of these elements, as they put it in a terminological formulation that gives up most of what must be made subject to theoretical disposition. And a disposition that can address this ongoing appearance, now well past the half-millennium mark, as we have already begun to recognize, was proposed by Du Bois from one end of his itinerary, its complex incipit in the midst of the 1890s, through to the closing steps of his discourse in the opening years of the 1960s. And, in addition, in a response to the initial statement of this trilogy, Giovanni Arrighi called attention to his own earlier clarification that from Marx's theorization of the indifference of capital to all members of the laboring classes, "one cannot infer as Marx does . . . a predisposition of labor to relinquish natural and historical differences" (Arrighi 2002, 19). One can notate here that Du Bois had already, in 1906, for example, specifically described such a bifurcation of the laboring classes in the United States across the last quarter of the nineteenth century in a pivotal sense due to a presumptive disposition by the "white" laboring classes according to a putative distinction along the so-called color line" (Du Bois 1906b; Du Bois 2006). Then, a quarter of a century later, in 1933, he proposed that to theorize this question, Marx's contribution on this point would have to be revised—a claim for revision that as we have just seen can be back dated to the opening of the First World War, if not more precisely to his work across the half-dozen years prior to that moment (namely, the closing chapters of his study of John Brown) (Du Bois [1933] 1983; Du Bois 1909; Du Bois 1973a). And, with reference to the American Civil War and its aftermath, he would later offer an extended form of such revision across the grand-scale narrative of his magnum opus *Black Reconstruction* (Du Bois 1935; Du Bois 1976a).) Is it not precisely the reinscription of the interest of the laboring classes, among others, of Europe and America, and now too the dominant economies of Asia, into forms of what Du Bois nearly a century ago called "democratic despotism" on a global scale that must still be engaged by theory as a persisting "paradox" in the contemporary organization of capital and the organization of social life in general in the twenty-first century?

With these references in mind, we now have in place the essential theoretical formulations such as to bring to summary relief the central contribution of *Color and Democracy: Colonies and Peace*. Two principal thetic lines are interwoven here. On the one hand, in essence, in the failure at the end of 1945 to address the matter of the colonies of Europe in a manner equal to other dispositions of the postwar order within the proposals to formulate a new United Nations, Du Bois was concerned that the forms of "democratic despotism" that he had adduced already during the advent of the First World War would be formalized in the institutions and instruments of global governance (forms, in which, as we have understood him to propose, in essence the laboring classes of the rich countries could join in the exploitation of the laborers of the poorer countries according to a principle of distinction that he gathered under the concept metaphor the "problem of the color line") (Du Bois 1945, 85; Du Bois 1975a, 85). It would formalize a hierarchy of nations and states at a juncture when the formal political and legal structures produced for a certain order of international governance in such relations could instead be transformed in an egalitarian matter based on the principle of democracy for the benefit of the whole world. On the other hand, as a historical corollary to his 1915 claim that imperial rivalry had set afoot the conflicts that led to the First World War, in this 1945 text he proposed that the failure to address the conditions of the colonies and to transform their position from their status in a prewar order, would lead to an unremitting source of conflict and war in the future (Du Bois 1945, 3–16, 100–114; Du Bois 1975a, 3–16, 100–114). In this pronouncement, Du Bois's perspective was undoubtedly the bearer of a practical-theoretical truth.

Here, it must be remarked as a kind of coda (at once epistemological and political) in our own time, that it is most fundamentally Du Bois's thought of the "problem of the color line" that subtends his thought for theoretical work in the midst of the complex contradictions of our contemporary globalization. For even if the most decisive processes and forms of institution in their tendency exceed the historical form of the national state, it remains that the horizon of differentiation remarked by Du Bois is still fundamentally at issue and must be theorized as such. While it may be transnational "corporations" (along with state sponsored corporations) that undertake "accumulation by dispossession" around the globe, in Africa, for example, this in and of itself proposes no dissolution of the structure of interest in the exploitation of the "colored" folks (a still powerfully viable metaphor because of its thematization of the supposedly unmarked, hence putatively empty, space of privilege) of the world on the part of all classes of the rich countries—as investors in such corporations (directly or indirectly)—that Du Bois had already formulated in 1915 and again in 1933. (This thought is at odds with the ambiguous formulations, as noted above, offered by Hardt and Negri, for example, in the concluding text of their signal theoretical trilogy for our time [Hardt & Negri 2009, cf. 203–48, esp. 231].) That is to say, the "problem of the color line" as thematized by Du Bois is the very form of the articulation of globalization, it is the very organization of such as a form of production of existence. It is a theoretical name for the organization of the very forces by which our contemporary horizons—of capitalism in all of its limits—is produced. Perhaps this is the possible meaning of the thought of postcolonial capitalism, or a constitutive transnational order of the most local and mundane forms of the lived sense of habitation, in our own time. In this sense, perhaps it should also name the epistemic horizon for new "historiographies and cartographies of global capitalism," as new "cultural demography," that would take as the mark of its own theoretical incipit the problem of producing a critical history of what I am proposing might be thought of as the colors of labor power, or what one might call a new Black studies—referencing with this latter term both sides of the Atlantic, certainly, but also a certain Asia (marked by the doubled parallaxes of both the Pacific Rim and the new yet so old rim of the Indian Ocean)—a certain horizon of the twenty-first century in Asia, Africa, the Americas, and Europe, and across "the islands of the sea" (Du Bois 1903d, 13, chap. 2, para. 1).

It is in this sense that we can remark the double title of the book. "Color and democracy," calls attention to the logic of differential production of the global scenography of peoples and states by that of the principle of "color prejudice" as a form of dividend in the wealthy countries at the expense of the poorer nations. "Colonies and peace," proposes that economic exploitation would serve, respectively, as a basis for rivalry among those states which would have the organization and authority to sustain it, on the one hand, and as a source of revolt, from those who would be exploited under the future systems of global governance as put forward at Bretton Woods, on the other. These two headings, in fact, represent simply different refractions of the same, common, problematic.

A Notation on Africa and Atopia. With this internal outline, so to speak, of Du Bois's formulation of the new imperial capitalist horizon for the production of the problem of the color line across the first half of the twentieth century, I can now turn to his configuration of an exemplary example in the torsion of this world history; it both extends and renders more complex the story as outlined thus far.

I give two annotations *here.*

First, I propose that this text, *The World and Africa* (one underscores its subtitle here—*"An Inquiry into the Part which Africa Has Played in World History"*) from 1947, is the epistemological equal of the 1935 text *Black Reconstruction: An Essay Toward a History of the Part which Black Folk Played in the Attempt to Reconstruct Democracy in America, 1860–1880* (Du Bois 1976a). Together they articulate the organization of Du Bois's most general reflections on modern historicity in the age of colonialism and modern imperialism. And this common status stands even as they are each realized according to quite different methodologies and orders of question. For each take their incipit from a common form of *theoretical* judgment: the character of a certain exemplarity of the example. However, second, it must also be indicated that Du Bois did not have here as a first order concern the project of rendering Africa a definite or constituted object of knowledge for a given form of truth or ensemble of such—disciplines.[8] Although, on another register he had proposed the necessity of such project for some four decades by the time of our 1947 text and, therefore, should nonetheless rightly be regarded as an epistemic pioneer in this domain (Du Bois 1975d).

Africa was for Du Bois an exemplary scene of an age old problematic that had in the modern era become fundamentally global. As he put it at the opening of his poignant closing chapter in *The World and Africa*, "Andromeda: Of the Future of the Darker Races and Their Relation to the White Peoples": it was "the basic problem of the relations of peoples" (Du Bois 1976d, 227). As we have noted, Du Bois was writing just after the formal conclusion of the Second World War. For him, the roots of that war stretched back to the inception of the Atlantic slave trade on the West Coast of Africa (and this perspective was an achieved one by the beginning of the First World War [Du Bois 1915]), set afoot on a global level in a distinctive problematic, the one that he had begun to formulate at the turn of the century as "the problem of the color line." This historical process was the inception of a specifically *modern* form of the imperial relation— here understood with a philosophical sense—in the torsion of gesture and recoil in which the modern projects of an affirmation of the *demos* were promulgated. In this sense the question of Africa's place in world history was an epistemic fulcrum according to which a certain fundamental order of modern historicity could be organized as a problem for thought. With that said, the epistemic sense here can be annotated a bit further. While, in one sense that order was and is a global history of the "problem of the color line" with which the practices of fascism in Europe and Asia in the twentieth century should be understood as continuous, even as the latter should also be understood as a decisive transformation within such practices on a global scale (and the turn to such absolutism—no matter its local and regional idiomatic mode—in one regime after another across the whole historical landscape of Africa since the advent of formal decolonization should be understood thus as continuous with this historicity), in another and prior sense, it concerns the immanent chance or freedom of irruptive possibility for futural forms of world—"beyond this narrow Now" (Du Bois 1903b, 213, para. 13). And while within an elaboration, a form of renarrativization of the practice of proscription, judgments can be made about the past and a program for the future can be reconceptualized, the sense of possibility that is at stake is more radical still. In this more radical sense, if understood as a certain kind of historically produced whole, that of a historial entity whose givenness is not absolute, Africa named for Du Bois both the limit of the modern practice of freedom and yet also the most poignant solicitation to a passage beyond it. Africa was both the scene of a world historical problematic and the name for a practical thought of *atopia*. It brought into view the farthest reaches of human practice in the past and in the future that would be yet to come. As such the world seen by way of the exemplary example of Africa—and in this sense it is yet still simply a mundane form for Du Bois, not greater and not less, in ontological terms, than any other—could be understood both in its historical form of limit in his present and yet also according to the radical possibility *of* an illimitable movement of freedom as historicity. It could yield then a simple and profoundly dispassionate and relativizing view of modernity as a historial movement and yet also allow the naming of the complex torsion by which all ideas of limit and hierarchy could be placed in radical question. Herein a certain acerbic and irreverent sense of history articulates itself within Du Bois's thought in the closing passage of the closing chapter of this book of *The World and Africa*.

> The continuity of a social group, the continuity of a civilization is at best doubtful and precarious. Most civilizations of the world have lasted less than three centuries, save Egypt. Even Egypt is only an apparent exception since, being for centuries without effective rivals, it did not actually collapse; but it changed so radically from age to age as to become almost a new land and culture. So too India and China lasted longer in name than in real cultural continuity. The broader the basis of a culture, the wider and freer its conception, the better chance it has for the survival of its best elements. This is the basic hope of world democracy. (Du Bois 1976d, 259)

And turning directly to the question of Africa itself as also the putting at stake of the future of the modern world (by way of a complicated reference to the Greek myth of Andromeda "the black daughter of Cepheus, King of Ethiopia and Cassiopea," a discussion of which in the proper sense I leave aside here (and such would entail considering the fact that twelve years earlier Du Bois concluded the narrative of *Black Reconstruction* with a figuration of "the black Prometheus bound to the Rock of Ages by hate hurt and humiliation, [who] has his vitals eaten out as they grow, yet lives and fights" [Du Bois 1976a, 670–709][9]), he will conclude this thought of its exemplarity, as the very closing lines of this concluding chapter, with the words: "the fire and freedom of black Africa, with the uncurbed might of her consort Asia, are indispensable to the fertilizing of the universal soil of mankind, which Europe alone never would or could give this aching earth" (Du Bois 1976d, 260). And, then in Beijing in 1959, just over a decade after the issuance of the first edition of *The World and Africa*, Du Bois would declare "Africa! listen to Asia" (Du Bois 1982b). Yet, just over half a century on, in our own moment, it should be underscored that it is now *also* China that turns expectantly to Africa, for resource as a necessary passage in the realization of its futural possibility, even as a certain Africa accepts with alacrity this embrace from China—all under the banner of a form of capital accumulation (and so, too, Japan and Korea). Yet, it must be asked: has not the imperial relation, as another refracting form of the "problem of the color line," been produced anew in this conjunction by the putatively sovereign form of the entrepreneurial relation of a state-led capitalism—as a distinct articulation of the new global-level order of finance capital—on the ground of one of the most entrenched loci of the historical formations of modern colonialism? If so, the operative question for a practical theoretical engagement should not be gathered under the heading of leadership, the question of sovereignty, but by way of a thought of the irruptive distanciation of such in the articulation of a relation to the past that is not simply given or already decided. What has gone by the name of China or Africa, respectively, for example, in all senses, but especially in a sense that we can call global or planetary, can no more be understood as simple or as one.[10] To respect this chance, as both freedom and necessity, is perhaps the most difficult difficulty for thought as practice in our time. Another order of historicity is announced therein, perhaps, other than the path of a simple or a one, a dimension that must be understood otherwise than according to the distinction of death from life and life from death, one in which the form of problem is only a name of that necessity which is possibility, while remaining in such a movement the formation of an opacity, by which that which is yet to come will always have been at stake.

Thus, finally, it can be said that while Du Bois's relation to Africa is often presented under the heading of kinship—apparently declared by him or by others for him—the thought of Africa's exemplarity indicates that his relation to this entity should be seen as a response to a solicitation that lead him to release from given shores of understanding and perspective. Just as the autobiographical example was for him something other than the story of his life, the historiographical example in its furthermost epistemic reach is something other than the narrative of a body, a family, or a kinship—whether in the restricted or extended senses of such metaphors. In this sense, for Du Bois, to think Africa's historiality was to simultaneously think the conditions and possibility of both his own existence—in all of its strange exemplarity—and likewise that of the modern world in general, in all of its persisting limits in the temporalities of its present. In this text, the figure of Africa proposed for Du Bois the problematization of modern historicity across the entirety of its immanent production, not only its pasts but also its futures, on the order of the question of possibility—at and beyond limit. For this reason, Africa remains in the life course of his thought not just a particular or parochial example but as also the hyperbolic name of a thought of a passage beyond limit in the existing sense of possibility of world. In this sense, the name of Africa in Du Bois's thought, serves as the heading for a formulation of problem that would not be reducible to a discrete place, a given topos, a fixed horizon—even as it remains tractable only according to an hypothesis of the movement of the formation of form.

Repassage

As the occasion of the incipit of a radical thought of the *utopic*, such problem is announced in the movement of the *atopic*—that is to say, not as a pure finality, but rather as the illimitable order of a movement that gives possibility as form.

And, further, it would announce itself as historial form, if at all, only in the movement "beyond this narrow Now"—in the maintenance of both sides of the limit—at the limit of world.

In a kind of epigraphic afterthought for the whole book called *The World and Africa*, one that stands beyond the close of the concluding chapter in the proper sense and which can thus be taken as a kind of hinge or fold linking the discourse of both this book and *Color and Democracy* to all of his subsequent thought, Du Bois remarks this extension of his thought of possibility within the figure of the human as rooted in a more radical order than the apparition of this figure. It bespeaks an affirmative thought of the inhuman, here as given in the figure of death, as other than a simple or an absolute, and as withdrawn from any judgment that would apprehend such devolution as a name for limit *or* possibility.

> Reader of dead words who would live deeds, this is the flowering of my logic: I dream of a world of infinite and invaluable variety; not in the laws of gravity or atomic weights, but in human variety in height and weight, color and skin, hair and nose and lip. But especially and far above and beyond this, in a realm of true freedom: in thought and dream, fantasy and imagination; in gift, aptitude, and genius—all possible manner of difference, topped with freedom of soul to do and be, and freedom of thought to give to a world and build into it, all

wealth of inborn individuality. Each effort to stop this freedom of being is a blow at democracy—that real democracy which is reservoir and opportunity and the fight against which is murdering civilization and promising a day when neither ". . . star nor sun shall waken, / Nor any change of light: / Nor sound of waters shaken / Nor any sound or sight; / Nor wintry leaves nor vernal, / Nor days nor things diurnal; / Only the sleep eternal / In an eternal night." There can be no perfect democracy curtailed by color, race, or poverty. But with all we accomplish all, even Peace. This is this book of mine and yours. (Du Bois 1976d, 261)[1]

While it could perhaps be acceptable to understand this closing epigraphic quotation of *The World and Africa*, which Du Bois takes from Swinburne's meditation on Persephone and the ancient Greek sense of underworld, as a kind of defiance of death, it is more profoundly thought as a complicated refusal of the sense of death as an absolute reduction to the same. Du Bois does not then deny death as such, but proposes a displacement of the practice of the sense of world that would attempt to *decide* world as a figure of the absolute. It is a complicated refusal of any claim of a sovereign right of exception to decide or determine the historial status of death. That is to say, it is a questioning of any practice that moves according to an always presumptive premise of a supposed authority for a peremptory violence. On the order of historical generality that he names as "civilization," Du Bois calls such presumption murder. And he remarks his withdrawal from it. This questioning of the authority of any practical-theoretical claim that would purport to be sovereign on the order of the historial is itself, perhaps paradoxically, put in motion by Du Bois's questioning of the figure of death on a metaphysical level as a simple absolute—as a so-called primordial other world, or underworld. Let us say that in this thought, death remains, even if such remains cannot be rendered as simply available under the heading of presence. This can be adduced if one allows the phrase "all manner of difference" its unsentimental remainder: whence such difference? And how? What might the *world* become? Who might *we* become? And if such becoming shows as simply a nodal passage of a movement or dimension beyond the "now" of historicity, whence or where is historial limit? Would not a received idea of *telos* as given in Greek conceptuality be put in question? If so, therein a simple yet exceedingly difficult thought of the reciprocity of origin and end could be announced: an elliptical, unstable, irregular rhythm that refuses as such to simply state or declare its theme—in which "the root of rhythm is its central unit of change" (Taylor 1966). The imperative at stake in Du Bois's statement here demands thus not so much a declaration of accession to the limit as it would call for a patient attention to the possibility of possibility, beyond even the modes of announcement of such, at once *atopic* in its movement and *utopic* in its implication.

Africa in the thought of Du Bois then is simply another heading— even as an exemplary one—for this problem of the maintenance of both sides of the limit.

At this juncture, then, certain dimensions of our supposed historicity—in its multiple afterlives of the past and its diverse rebirths of possible futures in the present—might be remarked. It remains that there has not yet been—and perhaps cannot be, in our time or those that we can yet imagine—any displacement of the problem of the centuries, that is, "the problem of the color line."

For, if it was Du Bois who in 1958, said to Africa look to Asia for your future, now, in our own moment, as we turn to search for a new horizon, might we not annotate that it is now the whole world, we might say, that is looking to Africa for *resource* in its gesture to announce itself anew on the new global horizon (the Africa that includes contemporary Tunisia, Egypt, and Libya, not, say, Algeria and Mauritania), just as a certain Europe did half a millennium past?

How might we understand this new yet old Asia in this still new millennium (Tsing 2005)? Whence this new China (Wong 1997; Pomeranz 2000; Arrighi 2007; Rosenthal & Wong 2011)? Does either or both remain open to, if such ever was truly the case, an *African* future, one that would be a new millennium of historicity for the world? And, if so, how?

And, on what terms, at what global cost, might a new Europe fail to begin to recognize itself in the new yet so old faces that are awash upon its shores (for the clamor they propose at the gates of detention—for example, in the wake of the Tunisian eruption, at Lampedusa off the southern coast of Italy—is also the tremulous voice of possibility, first as claim and then as potential practice, the practice of the potential, which may stand here as a general name for the generativity of the colors of labor power, beyond the limits of capitalization)?

Likewise, is this not still the question for all that has been called "America?" Here then, perhaps I can let stand—as a certain gathering of my thetic guide in this essay as a whole as it pertains to the figure of "America"—a quotation from the opening paragraph of the opening chapter of Du Bois's biography of John Brown, for not only does it situate the itinerary of that figure squarely within the productivity of Africa in America, it announces a radical and general, if still an unacknowledged, promissory (as indexed, at the very least, in certain declarations and constitutional claims made to the nations of the world under that name amid the advent of the new modicums of democratization of the eighteenth century) that subtends as the only sustainable path of all that is best in "America" into the centuries of the future that remain yet to come.

> The mystic spell of Africa is and ever was over all America. It has guided her hardest work, inspired her finest literature, and sung her sweetest songs. Her greatest destiny—unsensed and despised though it be—is to give back to the first of continents the gifts which Africa of old gave to America's father's fathers. Of all inspiration which America owes to Africa, however; the greatest by far is the score of heroic men whom the sorrows of these dark children called to unselfish devotion and heroic self-realization: Benezet, Garrison, and Harriet Stowe; Sumner, Douglass and Lincoln—these and others, but above all, John Brown. (Du Bois 1973a: 15; Du Bois 1909, 1)

And this is a nominalization to which we would be led to add: Fannie Lou Hammer, Martin Luther King Jr., Ella Baker, and Malcolm X, for example. By way of an "African" reference then, might we understand "America" *not only* as a derivative production of the historicity named under the heading of the African American situation, that is as an exemplar of the tendentious unfolding of the global "problem of the color line," that is, of limit within history, but also of possibility, at and beyond the limit of the as yet impossible possible world?

Is not the question then, can our planet-wide historicity affirm a new sense of Africa—or a new sense of "Blackness," or a new sense of the "colors" of a future world—and hence a new sense of *the* world, which is to say there will never have been only one? Might we reimagine the possible exemplars of the heterogeneous possibility of any supposed ultimate form of whole on the order of the historial?

Could such a form of question offer a new practical-theoretical sense of what has for so long been the *problem* of the color line as instead a name for illimitable possibility—of difference, diversity, dispensation, development, and most radically *new forms of engenderment*—in brief, a new sense of democracy to come (Davis 1998; Spillers 2003a; Butler 2004)?

Can we think such a thought within and beyond—toward a new sense of the future—of what has for too long been given to the name "philosophy" (Gordon 2008; Silva 2007; Moten 2003)?

If I may propose the demand for such a thought, let me then say all too briefly: why not call it the "Black horizon," the "new worlds of color," or even (if we think it as a name for the human in general) an "African future," as well as an "Asian century"?

Or, perhaps we should simply remark it as the centuries of color to come. For, in all truth, it remains the great myth in our time that there are people(s) without "color." Yet, who, or what, will not always have been only an example of such?

Perhaps then it is not too much to say that what comes into relief when we think with Du Bois in the manner—following the question of "color," Blackness, or an African future, shall we say—that I have proposed herein is a sense of limit and possibility that might go beyond the impasse of a contemporary discussion that still presumes the possible projection of a singular horizon for thought—usually in the form of an imperial Europe or European America, but now too on occasion in the form of a sovereign and leading China (just as such an order of thought was once proposed by according Japan as such example)—as definitive of the terms of theoretical problematization. It may be that an apparently parochial formulation of problem by way of the necessary and self-critical exposure of the limits of both its possibility and its becoming is more resolute *and* supple in its guide for critical thought in our time than one that would propose to accede directly to the limit and announce its discourse as the ultimate form of passage beyond such. A certain form of tarrying with the partial might well name in a felicitous manner the most intractable difficulties posed for thought in our time. If so, it proposes a certain patient restlessness in the promulgation of thought as theoretical practice. It maintains within its elaboration a responsibility that would not disavow its emergence according to the limit that it would seek to engage. Yet it also, by way of that very maintenance, inhabits a protocol that recognizes and insists on the always previous responsibility of its impossible responsibility in the present to a possibility that remains yet to come. In this complicated practice it would remain open to its own limit as the very form of its becoming. In this sense the passage beyond the limit for thought as practice is only according to the always immanent announcement of its own heterogeneity in its possible becoming otherwise than the given. Passage, if there is such, remains never only absolute. Possibility otherwise is never simply given. Affirmation of such, as a practice, maintains thereby its own critical form of responsibility to both sides of the limit as the terms by which historicity gives possibility.

All this is certainly both an old and yet a new horizon for thought—immanence as both limit and becoming—here understood from that *atopic* nonplace far beyond the thought of death as a form otherwise than being.

Annotation I

In the same manner that he had proposed an essay for understanding the historical world in the immediate aftermath of the First World War in *Darkwater: Voices from Within the Veil* (1920a), wherein, as he declared in its preface, that work was issued by way of his taking resource within the standpoint of a "veiled" corner, adducing a global-level reference thereby from the African American sense of world, a sense that he placed under the inimitable heading of a kind of historical "double-consciousness," as he had put it a generation earlier, in *The Souls of Black Folk: Essays and Sketches* of 1903, so too at the denouement of the Second World War, within the frame of a text that he inscribed under the heading *Color and Democracy: Colonies and Peace* (1945), Du Bois came to propose a careful critical account of the planetary-level epochal devastation produced as another "world war" and its aftermath (Du Bois 1920b; Du Bois 1975b; Du Bois 1903d; Du Bois 1945; Du Bois 1975a).

In his 1945 text, Du Bois produced a reelaboration of the tragic, yet hopeful sense that he had proffered a generation earlier, in 1920. However, the tragic sense that attended his ruminations in the wake of the First World War, marked at that time especially by a sense of loss was now resituated at the end of the Second World War (even as it remained legible) as a prophetic judgment oriented by and toward a sense of the future.

It is a discourse, across seven chapters, that issued at once as a general historiographical-sociological inquiry, a moral petition or appeal to the highest of values, that is to say ideals, and as a practical-theoretical declaration of truth.

After a preface that offers the whole of the book in capsule form, true to habitual style for Du Bois, whether in essay or book form, but less in narrative than economical concept, presented yet in an everyday almost reportorial locution, Du Bois proceeds in the opening chapter on the conference at Dumbarton Oaks in Georgetown (in the District of Columbia) to, set in place the sense of occasion of the event of a preparatory discussion for a new global-level international political and economic order, in the wake of the Second World War. Above all, he presents it as a scene of exclusion, that nonetheless, without declaration, he is able to read, for himself and for us, and perhaps for the majority of peoples of the earth, not only in the present of the time of occurrence of that specific event, but of those not yet afoot within the world, those generations to come. The great powers—the governments of the Allied Powers, as well as the avatars of the vanquished, have excluded him and those like him, the actual historical majority of the peoples of the earth, but especially those we might understand as Negro or African American from any pertinence to the discussion at hand. However, the pivotal matter at hand: it included the premise of an agreement to create a "United Nations organization," yet included no consideration of the status of "peoples" of colonies; indeed, the discussion in plan as well as practice did not include any provision for their direct involvement in the discussion in their own name, so to speak.

There follows two chapters presenting a conception of the kinds of "peoples" of the world comprising this diverse majority across the world. They are two kind: those within "disfranchised colonies" (the major part of this majority), and the "unfree peoples" (a differentiated but distinctly contiguous extension of and within this worldwide majority.

There follows the turning point chapter of the whole book, its center weight, in both conception and narrative elaboration. It articulates Du Bois's conception of democracy in the world, in terms of its articulation of and in relation to his majority. The chapter gives its title to the book *Color and Democracy*, but here in performative statement, as the chiasmic expression of the book title. It is "color," as metaphor, that stakes the kinetic force of Du Bois's argument with the powers that be. What the metaphor specifies will be the substance of the argument of the book. Yet, in the chapter title, his concern, "democracy," conceived and named as the ultimate concern of the book is presented as an unqualified universal, to which one can hardly maintain reserve at the historical time of his presentation of his statement. It announces a concern that is or ought to be unassailable within the historical apparition of its first locution.

Then comes three chapters, which eventually bring the book to a close, that each argue in distinct ways that a peace—in the sense of world history of the long term—will be determined on the basis of the promulgation of self-determination on the part of the "colonized" and as yet "unfree" peoples of the world. By 1945, "Russia," in all its enigmatic and yet world-historical status, since the revolutions of the first years of the century and its ambivalent yet epoch-making role in the defeat of European fascism, within the previous half-dozen years (to the time of Du Bois's writing) is for him the odd one—in all senses, at 1945, which way or ways will it go? W. E. B. Du Bois at the end of 1944 is distinctly hopeful, just as he had been in the 1920s, and the 1930s, and would remain so through the 1940s, of what the new "Russia" might offer to the coming world. Most especially, the question that may be understood to move in an uncertain tone and register on the lower frequencies of this text is—what will be the relation of this Russia to Asia, at once China and Japan, but also Korea?

Arched in its delivery on the basis of a rather resolute sense of authority and accomplished understanding—an authority that is assumed according to an ordination without any subordination—as such, the 1945 text was also marked by a robust and resonant sobriety.

The voice from this text as it addressed the reader spoke both from and for the whole of humankind—at once partial in its assumed responsibility, for persons and groups demarcated by "color," as he staked the metaphor, and limited by contemporary colonialism, as he specified the historicity, and impartial, in its prophetic implication, for any and all across the future, yet to come, that might be considered as of the human.

This 1945 book, *Color and Democracy*, issues forth under the heading of an ideal, one that has been determined prior to the project of the book itself: the value of "the permanent abolition of war" (as Du Bois formulated it in his proposal for the book that he presented to the publisher Harcourt, Brace at the end of November 1944) (Aptheker 1975, 6).

The main thesis of the book is that such peace, supposed as permanent in principle, or even a sustained or long-lasting peace, on a worldwide basis would be possible only under a general and tendentiously universal practice of democracy, that is, across the whole of planet earth and all that it might entail. There will be no peace without the realization of democracy on a worldwide scale.

There are three supporting, or corollary theses that subtend the main thesis of the book.

The first corollary is that the maintenance into the future, beyond 1945, of a centuries-long tendentious, general colonial premise—as projected from Western Europe across the modern epoch—will render null the prospect of democracy on a worldwide and world-historical scale of reference. In historical terms, at the opening of 1945, for Du Bois, "the greatest opponent of democracy was "imperial colonialism," rather than fascism (and the reference here is general, and not only to Europe). Alternatively stated, in the terms of an immediate contemporaneous historical reference, operating from an imperial and colonial premise, "democracy in Europe may continue to impede and nullify democracy in Asia and Africa" (Du Bois 1975a, 228). "[C]olonial imperialism" will remain a "continual cause of other wars in the century to come" (Du Bois 1975a, 112–13). Here, I propose that this premise may be understood as a practical presumption of categorical difference, hence hierarchy, among humankind, articulated by Du Bois as the essential predication of a global-level "problem of the color line." In theoretical terms, we can spell out two aspects of Du Bois's conception of problem, as adduced in the text of *Color and Democracy*. The first is that it entails the entire complex of thought and practice gathered according to the idea and concept of race, of distinction among humans, according to a determination of mark called or nominalized as "race." The second, is that the entire complex of theses of his disposition—toward the outcome that he seeks—presumes the accomplishment in thought and understanding (actively and self-reflectively, and not just passively) of the premise (or value of, the truth of) an idea, a judgment of both knowledge and value, of "racial equality" (Du Bois 1980c, 385).

The second corollary is that as of late Autumn of 1944 and early winter of 1945, "European civilization" can no longer stand as the norm, or measure, of the idea and practice of democracy on a world historical order of understanding.

Given in the preface of *Color and Democracy*, which is dated to the first day of the year, the articulate emergence of this judgment of value, at once moral and historial, as a term of Du Bois's understanding of both Europe, in particular, and the world, in general, bespoke the self-reflexive (and thus critical) configuration an entire decades-long a tendentious understanding modern historicity on his part, which had been first decisively inflected by the onset of the First World War. Then, well beyond the eruption and ongoing maelstrom of the opening years of the Second World War, the time during which Du Bois is completing his writing is astride a pivotal moment of modern historicity, of war; the weeks of the last major offensive by Germany under Hitler, at which Ardennes may be taken as axial, prior to the last stand of the Nazi regime at Berlin of the spring of 1945; and then the unprecedented aerial bombardment of cities across Japan (at least sixty-five cities, by the time of the declaration of an armistice to end the war), during that same time frame, before the battle at Okinawa, and then the American deployment of the devastation of the unheard of—previously unimaginable—nuclear weapons on two locations on the archipelago in August of 1945. Du Bois's adjudgment came to historical theoretical understanding and voice just prior to this historical moment. There are two specifications that should receive our attention here. As of the opening of 1945, for him, no modern nation or state at that time could be considered truly democratic. Nazi Germany was not original. Rather, on the one hand, they followed premises cultivated over the previous five centuries and more of the imperial powers of Europe, from the mid-fifteenth century, especially since the sixteenth. (This thought stands as the historical reference for the opening three chapters of *The World and Africa*, published in 1947). On the other hand, Germany specifically took over and generalized the American example, with regard to both Native Americans and Africans, enslaved across the North American subcontinent, as Americans, directed specifically against persons of Jewish tradition and family descent, and Judaism as practice, along with the Roma of Europe, as well as others (Du Bois 1975a, 91). Notably, Du Bois, provides the distinct reference that organized labor, in Europe and in the United States, did not take a general principle of opposition to imperialism. (This thought by Du Bois goes all the way back to the turn to the twentieth century, as I remarked above in my initial discussion of his thought of the "problem of the color line.") At best, perhaps, another or new Europe, or a new America, might join another vision of a new and democratic world; however, at 1945, Du Bois was no longer looking to Europe as a source for such practical imagination. Eventually, he would come to take reserve from the practical engagement of "America," following the decade and a half or more immediately after the cessation of the Second World War.

The third corollary is the practical theoretical judgment by Du Bois that at the end of the world debacle of the mid-century war on a new worldwide scale of reference, another exemplar of value and norm, or alternatively said, another example of premise, with regard to the human was necessary for the realization of true democracy. That is, the judgment based on several terms of reference, taken as several conditions, for thought and action. These conditions and judgment that follows therefrom are the presumed virtue of the idea of democracy in tandem with the circumstance that the previous presumptive and thus leading example of such idea could no longer be taken as exemplary, as the exemplar. In addition, Du Bois concluded that there are sources for new norms: the diverse majority of peoples of the world, that is, from the colored peoples of the world ("worlds of color").

Finally, thus, the diverse majority of groups of people across the planet must become "copartners" in a new project of worldwide democracy. This bespeaks theoretical possibility. Yet, on the same order of problem, another sense of the conditions that give determination to theoretical practice, yielded practical limits, according to relation of human forms of well-being to techne (in all senses of doing or making, fabrication, technologies of living), including not only basic, fundamental, preparation or training for life, but the improvement, the refashioning, or even perfectibility, of the human by way of education, this latter understood as in principle illimitable. In direct historical terms, Du Bois named two such conditions, in specific: the relief of "poverty," by which above all he meant the "economic" means of life; and "education," namely, the provision of free public education, in general, for all, on a worldwide basis, among all human beings over the course of the future century and more (after 1945). Eventually, Du Bois will spell the specific conditions of the moment, that must be directly and immediately henceforth overcome in order for general world-historical democracy to find its way; that along with the "abolition" of poverty, and the promulgation of education, health (mainly understood as physical, but with no declared withdrawal from a concern with the mental or emotional) and freedom from "disease," and finally "security" (and he names, but does not elaborate, the "scientific treatment of crime"). The most fundamental dimension of this practical theoretical aspect of Du Bois's thought here has to do with the sense temporality at stake in his conception. Du Bois is concerned about the future. Hence his judgment of the relative status of possibility and limit with regard to the historicity at stake in his time, is oriented toward that which remains yet to come (and not so much that which has been or may continue to be, as it were). Thus, for Du Bois, the extension of democracy should be concerned less with defense (of rights and status, of circumstance), although it must include such. And the presence of the aggression and hostilities, and mass murder of the Second World War stood as proof of the need for such protections. Rather, his deepest concern arose from his judgment that the elaboration of democracy would liberate capabilities within any and all that might be understood as human that had never yet been realized, and in practical principle could emerge as illimitable. To enable, affirm, this sense of possibility may be understood as the guiding thought of this book of Du Bois, as he signed its preface at the opening of January 1945.

It may serve us in our overall thought to recall the three dimensions of discourse that are interwoven in the locutions of this text. It is at once an inquiry, an appeal, and a new sense of a declaration. It is an inquiry that entailed what most certainly a half century later would be remarked under the heading of the field of postcolonial studies. As an appeal it recalls the discourse of rights of the seventeenth and eighteenth centuries of Europe and the Americas, notably including the Caribbean with the latter, even as it yet proposed a radical extension of any practice that we may place under the heading of a humanism, beyond any and all extant liberalism—that is, toward an inclusion that reemplaces all past practices within a form of exorbitance that has radically changed itself and all that was once thought to absorb it. As a declaration, at once political and economic, one that can no longer be placed under the heading of "independence," for in all truth a dependence on the part of the colonized was never the order of the day, but an expression and articulation beyond the horizon that might be possible according to any imperial impulse, even in thought, as an explanation of any supposed common—as in the idea of a commonwealth—or the multiple; for, articulation of ipseity has never emerged, or arrived, on the order of the simple, the one, or the absolute singular. The historicity at stake here has always been heterogeneous in both its genesis and its possible ways of becoming, and for being at stake for the future.

Annotation II

The text of *The World and Africa: An Inquiry into the Part which Africa Has Played in World History* was composed during and immediately following that fateful year of the twentieth century and world history, 1945—after the devastation unleashed at Hiroshima and Nagasaki by the first and only use of nuclear weapons in warfare, and thereafter the legal cessation of the hostilities marked as the declared end of the Second World War, the Great Pacific War (Du Bois 1947; Du Bois 1976e).

The singularity of its conception and locution in the itinerary of W. E. B. Du Bois is not that of an exception. Rather, it is the expression in its epitome of the form of the historical conceptualization of the formation and eventuality of modern historicity, that is—world history on a planetary-wide scale of reference from the middle of the fifteenth century through the middle of the twentieth. In that conception, the historicity of Africa, conceived by Du Bois as a global historical reference, at once immemorial and contemporary, has been an essential, indeed constitutive, condition of its emergence, itinerary or perdurance, an exemplary example of the reciprocal articulation of both its limit and its possibility, always though in the plural, in each instance. For Du Bois, to think the historicity of the modern world without Africa would be the unthinkable, itself.

As borne out within that text, after 1945 Du Bois came to the judgment that on a planetary-wide basis, humankind had need of a fundamentally different, if not entirely new, horizon of ideals, indeed of the highest order of ideals and idealization of value, of morals, and principles of collective social practice. In Du Bois's estimation, the historicity of Africa marked out an exemplary domain for the recognition of resource for such other ways of idealization.

For Du Bois, this conception of Africa was through and through in historical consort—at once economic, political, demographic, and "philosophical"—with Asia. The latter certainly included the domain we today place under the appellation "China," but so too "India," and then notably also "Japan," on par with those two exemplars (shall we say, in the historial sense). However, more broadly, it was in all truth the whole or entirety of Asia as a broad and open ended domain of originary historial emergence and perdurance, multiple and quite far-flung, not at all as simply something other and alien to his sense of Africa, that marked the radical heterogeneity thereof as itself internal, as it were (diverse and of diversity) that Du Bois found so persuasive. For Du Bois, as he titled the most enigmatic chapter in the text *The World and Africa*, according to his sense of both genesis and possibility there was already a reciprocal articulation of "Asia in Africa." For, as Du Bois wrote it,

> The connection between Asia and Africa has always been close. There was probably an actual land connection in prehistoric times, and the black race appears in both continents in the earliest records, making it doubtful which continent is the point of origin. Certainly the Negroid people of Asia have played a leading role in her history. . . . So for a thousand years Asia and Africa strove together, renewing their spirits and mutually fertilizing their cultures from time to time, in West Asia, North Africa, the Nile Valley, and the East Coast [of Africa]. (Du Bois 1976e, 176–200, quotations at 176 and 200, brackets mine)

The sense here may be understood as notwithstanding that for him, "Africa" itself—in Du Bois's sense of the nomination—has been the very immemorial name and the autochthonous scene of the emergence of the human as kind, in general.

As annotated earlier, Africa appears in the title for book's closing chapter under the heading of the metaphorical figure "Andromeda," from ancient Greek mythology. As the story is told—in order to forego a foretold destruction for all (Greeks, humans) due to an act of hubris in the face of the gods—Andromeda was "chained and exposed on a headland facing the sea." "Andromeda" in Du Bois's telling is Africa. So, too, then, "Africa" is humankind. Then, the penultimate sentence of the book proper is that "Andromeda" must be released from her chains—and take a rightful place among the stars, in "the great heaven" (Du Bois 1976e, 226–69, quotations at 226 and 260).

My annotation at this juncture in discourse is formulated as a brief practical-theoretical enunciation between these two apostrophes, the beginning and end, as it were, of this mythological storytelling.

The guiding premise of this book is that Africa is of the highest value to world civilization, both past and future. Of the past, in Du Bois's understanding at the time of his writing, from 1945 to 1947, there is a profound history, of which a historiography is possible, of an original and originary "Negroid" African genesis. Of the future, Du Bois proposes that Africa may be thought of as a name for an affirmation of difference by way of democracy, in general, and in principle. As the preparation for a conception of a practical theoretical program for the release and the promotion of the figure of "Black" "Andromeda"—by an atopic metaphorical extension, we may also annotate this nomination as remarking the formerly "colonized," or also the "colored" peoples, of the world—this is the real concern of the book. That is, Du Bois is ultimately concerned with how to approach the future of the world in the wake of the disaster that had reached the articulation of an historical crescendo in 1945, across the previous half dozen years, on a world-historical basis of reference.

The question might have been put thus: is there hope for the youth of the world?

On a more mundane level, Du Bois's book may be understood as a general theoretical testament. It is an interpretation of the historicity of the modern epoch, thought as a kind of whole. If so, then we might remark on two indices: (1) the present limit of the status of a supposed European civilization, or what had gone forth so far under that name, for that future; and (2) the present possibility of an "African" genesis (if one might tolerate such a name) of ideals (for such a future). This latter, would be despite or otherwise than the exemplary status of past possibility, notably of the renaissance or resurgence of the beneficence of "ancient" accomplishment— from the time of the historial opening that was Kush and Ethiopia (not to gainsay Egypt) to the time of the historial opening of the Song dynasty on the mainland of China (both Northern Song and Southern Song, and neither—no differentiation among them, at this level—as an ipseity), across a temporality of some four and a half millenniums and more, as showing forth within any sense of the modern, say of the previous half-millennium and more, at the time of Du Bois's writing, in 1945. So too, this latter ("Africa" as a present and future name for possibility) would be despite and beyond the ineluctable imperatives that formed by way of loss and destruction in the past, notably all that has been and continues to entail through the historicity of modern systems of enslavement on a global scale.

The key aspect of Du Bois's conception of Africa for the future is its diversity, at every level, all the way up and all the way down, so to speak. In a theoretical sense that is commensurate with the conceptualization of "The Message," the postscript that closes the 1947, first edition of the book, which we noted above, this diversity has two senses: of resource (both potential and possible), and of realization (the illimitable sense of what can be given by way of the resources that might be brought forth from "Africa").

If there is a singularity that attends to Africa, for Du Bois, it is resolutely historical and (in a nonparadoxical sense) relative. It is a singular heading for multiplicity (if thought by way of metaphor from index to a mathesis), or better, differences (if thought it terms of a genesis, a genetics and a radical thought of any futural disposition that may be remarked as genealogical). The matter here may be understood with regard to the demands of any thesis, any thetic practice, or theoretical intervention: in order for there to be the emergence of the novel, it is necessary for a certain displacement and a form of kinetic overturning of the given terms of reference for the articulation of a way other than the assumed, accepted, or presumed, most precisely if what has been given manifests as a form of originary violence—that is the withholding or foreclosing of the as yet impossible forms of the possible. There must be an overturning, a kind of making low of what was once the high. Or, better said: there must be the apparition of a singular thesis in order to produce that overturning. I have given this thought a theoretical exposition with regard to the example of the itinerary and practice of W. E. B. Du Bois as it pertains to the concept of difference among the human, in the context of the question of the "Negro," in America, at the turn to the twentieth century (Chandler 2014a, 40–56).

Across the first three chapters of *The World and Africa*, under the impress of one premise, Du Bois gives three critical indices with regard to knowledge and thought as to how to understand the historicity that is his concern. That premise is that the promulgation of modern enslavement is the "prime and effective cause of the contradiction" and "collapse" of "European" (which includes within than remark, a certain disposition of or from an "American") "civilization" (Du Bois 1976e, 27). Those three indices are: (1) that Africa is an originary genesis on a worldwide scale of reference (this index will later in the text be elaborated across chapters 4 to 10); (2) the systems of the enslavement of Africa in the modern period were constitutively revolutionary in the emergence of modern-world historicity on a planetary basis (this is most concisely put in chapters 2–3, within this text); and (3) the status of the historial profile of Europe, as the name of a modern historial entity is (a) constitutively produced from a historicity in common with the itinerary of these systems of enslavement, and (b) that historicity cannot be considered as an unmitigated or uncritical source of norms of any judgment of the world-historical status of value (or better, values as ideals), not only for Africa, in principle (that is, neither in any particularity, nor in general), but most especially not for any supposed sense of the world in general (likewise as Du Bois's text puts the matter in chapters 2–3).

In terms of the itinerary and theoretical historiographical practice of W. E. B. Du Bois, these opening three chapters of *The World and Africa* of 1947 may be understood to stand in theoretical contiguity with the opening three chapters of *Black Reconstruction* of 1935, for they each establish the constitutive historial figure of the "Black" or "colored" worker (as enslaved, freed, "colonized, and—by full extension of the concept-metaphor—also this reference includes contemporaneous worker-members of those countries that Du Bois understood as an "unfree" modern state), to the formation of a global system of historical (mundane, eventual) and historial (ontological, existential) production, at once economic and political, not to gainsay all that can placed as "cultural") in the concomitant elaboration of the deriv-ative formation of systems of hierarchy and ordination in which a figure supposed (by itself and others) as an historical "white" entity, whether as "white worker," "planter," "colonizer," or "capitalist" (Du Bois 1976e, 1–97; Du Bois 1976a, 3–54). In each context, Du Bois's thought is operating on a historiographical plane of reference that ought be understood as international, global, indeed planetary, that is, in its conceptual and theoretical projection.

Thereby we may take note that the first three chapters of *The World and Africa* are a summation of the theoretical perspective of modern histo-ricity that Du Bois had been tendentiously developing since the early 1890s (as one may note in the recent posthumously published text of circa 1894, titled "The Afro-American," which reached a nodal general formulation and expression in the early essay of 1900, "The Present Outlook for the Dark Races of Mankind" (widely underread, as I note above) (Du Bois 2010; Du Bois 2015a; Du Bois 1900; Du Bois 2015d). A signal reference at the onset of the First World War, as noted above, is Du Bois's essay "The African Roots of War" (Du Bois 1915). While, indeed, the text *Color and Democracy: Colonies and Peace* (annotated above) was the first full-scale book-length historiographical and sociological disposition and deployment of that theoretical perspective, which directly and specifically names the worldwide scale of its reference as its immediate concern, the novel *Dark Princess* from

1928, had already proposed a fictional narrative on this historical scale of indication (even as the latter was necessarily centered on a "character" as the cipher that connects the different dimensions of the problematic at stake) (Du Bois 1975a; Du Bois 1928; Du Bois 1974a). Likewise, although seldom recognized, the entire weight of the theoretical bearing that attends to the text issued as *Black Reconstruction* of 1935 pertains to its historiographical pertinence as a study of one of the two exemplary examples of the irruption of democracy within, and yet potentially beyond, the limits of the paths of the global "problem of the color line" in the Americas, the role of "Black folk" in the devolution of the American Civil War and its aftermath (Du Bois 1976a).

The other example, with such world-historical status (with a singularity all its own), was the revolution that resulted in the declaration of Haiti, as a historial entity (Du Bois 1961; Du Bois 1962; Du Bois 1970).

The temporality that is the concern of *The World and Africa* is not so much the past—even as more than 80 percent of the book, perhaps, is about the past—as it is about the future. It imagines another order of referential indexes for the past, most certainly. Yet, the kinetic force of Du Bois's writing and the reassembly of passages of this thought from the past, from across almost the entirety of the widely deployed and multiple mediums of his writing—as journalist and scholar, as well as fiction writer and indefatigable public orator, for example—is to find ways of articulating visions of the future that are different than those of his historical present. Stated in apparently simple terms: the ultimate concern of the text is how to imagine the future, for the whole of the world, as such.

Herbert Aptheker gave us the annotation that W. E. B. Du Bois first wrote to Viking Press about the possibility of their publishing the text that would eventually become *The World and Africa* on the seventeenth of January 1945, the day after he sent the corrected manuscript of *Color and Democracy* to Harcourt, Brace (both of which presses had major offices located in New York City, wherein he also resided at that time) (Aptheker 1975, 5). The initial title that Du Bois proposed to Viking Press for the book was "The Africas." He wished to focus on the question of Africa "at the time of the first World War, since that war, [and] during the present war, with a forecast of what is going to happen in Africa after this war" [brackets mine]. He proposed "a small book" of 150–200 pages. Within three weeks, following a positive response from then president of Viking Press, B. W. Huebsch, on the 23rd of January and a ten-paragraph outline of the proposed book, in turn in reply, from Du Bois to the Press the following day, by the 13th of February, 1945, a contract for the book had been signed between Du Bois and the Press and an advance was delivered to Du Bois (Aptheker 1976, 8).

At the very end, in the last paragraph of the last item, of his ten-paragraph outline of the proposed book, Du Bois states that the book, with the previous paragraphs outlining much the potential content that would speak to the concerns that he had named in his initial inquiry to Viking Press, with regard to the temporal terms in question, that is, the past, present, and future of Africa, Du Bois stated what could well be taken as the guiding epistemological thought of his whole project. He stated that to properly address the question of "what now is the future of this continent . . . the cultural status and contributions of Africans must be scientifically studied and used for the emancipation of the continent" (Aptheker 1976, 8). Its legible appearance at the end of the statement ought not belie its epistemological status or its pertinence for the theoretical project of this book. For it can be shown that in the book this formulation stands as its grounding premise. (The operative sense of premise, such as I understand it here is that of a presupposition that stands outside of and prior to both the conception and the theoretical practice of the book itself. Further, the conception formulates the object of the book, what it is about. The theoretical practice of the book is the manner of explanation that is carried forth about such an object, or topic, of concern.) This order of premise in all truth is not made subject to any direct contention, for the author, despite appearances. Rather, the truth of such premise is exhibited in a rather relentless fashion, everywhere, and always, within, indeed as the very text itself. Its truth, the truth of this premise, is more performed than debated. From this grounding premise comes the other key premise of the book, we might say its thetic premise (for it emerges as the very contention or declared intervention in thought and knowledge that would be—or in fact is—argued, placed at stake, in the book in itself). That premise, namely, is the "importance of Africa to modern world." This importance has two immediate forms: on the one hand, Africa's astounding economic status as resource (of all kinds) and, on the other, its demographic diversity as capacity (which ought to be understood as "cultural," as well genetic-genealogical, thus in this latter sense also as notably not only "biological"). There is a corollary thetic premise, which I have already annotated above: the necessity that Africa, and by metaphoric extension, the world in general, turn away from "European" ideals as any kind of singular or supposed preeminent guide to the promulgation of collective values for the future, on a planetary basis.

Although Du Bois proposed in mid-February 1945 to his publisher that he would work to finish the book by June of 1945, historical events, both worldwide and personal, intervened to contravene that projection by Du Bois. On the personal: Du Bois was appointed in April of 1945, to the delegation of the National Association for the Advancement of Colored People's (NAACP's) inaugurating conference for the specific formation of the United Nations organization; in the autumn, Du Bois became intensely involved in the preparation of the Fifth Pan-African conference, along with his close attention to matters of negotiating-the-peace following the conclusion of the hostilities of the Second World War (both in Europe and in general). Arriving in London from late October, Du Bois would remain in Europe through the very last days of December 1945. On the world historical: the final offensives of the Second World War unfolded throughout the middle months of that year. The multiple offensives of the Allies, including Russia, led to the "official" surrender of Germany in early May of 1945. After nearly six months of an almost unprecedented incendiary bombardment on cities throughout the archipelago, and the famous battle of Okinawa, the deployment of nuclear weapons, by the United States at Hiroshima and Nagasaki, led to the formal surrender of Japan on August 15, 1945.

It was not until the month following his return from London to New York, that from early January to the month of March 1946, Du Bois prepared his first complete draft of the text that became *The World and Africa*—now with a new title for the book (different than his original one). During the months of May and June 1946, Du Bois redrafted the text, producing a book that was completely rewritten, almost a new book. Then, across the summer months of July and August of 1946, assisted notably by the scholar Irene Diggs (working as an assistant to Du Bois at that time), and in collaboration with the production staff at Viking Press, Du Bois realized a final version of the text, and submitted to the press in early September of that year. The book was released for publication in January of 1947 (Aptheker 1976, 9).

Annotation III

Two essays, one written during the time of the composition of the book *The World and Africa*, and the other written after its completion (this latter essay reflecting in its claim the articulations of both *The World and Africa* and *Color and Democracy*, indeed, formulating precisely their mutual articulation), ought be recognized here.

The first, is an essay on the pan-African movement, "The Pan-African Movement," written in 1945 and published in a volume edited by George Padmore, which is essentially Du Bois's declaration of personal provenance with regard to the idea of pan-Africanism, as a distinctive twentieth century intellectual and political projection (Du Bois 1982d). This text was drafted just prior to Du Bois's participation in the historic Fifth Pan-African conference at Manchester in October of 1945.

The other, "A Program of Emancipation for Colonial Peoples," is an essay that might well stand as a lucid summary revision of the argument of *Color and Democracy*, two years on, in the form of a singular, lithe, locution, which thereby could easily be taken as a kind of appeal, addressed to all those who might listen in the name of the project of the newly formed and forming organization of the United Nations (Du Bois 1982e).

Throughout the year of 1944, and the first half of 1945, at least three major intellectuals of the African Diaspora—Rayford W. Logan, Amy Jacques Garvey, and George Padmore, among others, prevailed on Du Bois to take the lead in the broad solicitation of commitment and participation of potential delegates to a fifth pan-African conference (after four previous ones, dating from the turn to the new century, in the year of 1900, to 1927). In October of 1945, a fifth such meeting was held in Manchester, England, with Du Bois, as the informal honorary chairperson.

"The Pan-African Movement," an essay by Du Bois, was published in a volume edited by Padmore. Although written after *Color and Democracy*, it was completed prior to the Manchester convocation. Spelled out across ten pages, Du Bois's discourse, at once a personal memoir and an informal organizational record, places him as the principal progenitor of the movement for pan-Africanism. In an essential sense that presentation is without contention. Doubtless, the scale and breadth of the movement over its first half-century bears historical witness to the depth and extent of the operative activity of many intellectuals and activists from around the whole of the Atlantic Basin and more. Yet, it is apposite here to note the principal basis of the activity annotated by Du Bois in his account: the project of the two most effectual conferences, at Paris in 1919 and at Manchester in 1945, took place on the occasion of the imagination of the possibility of a fundamental reorganization of the relation of matters of the continent of Africa to both Europe and a postwar international economic and political order—following each of the World Wars, respectively. In other words, what was entailed was the status of all that we may call colony, with regard to Africa, proper. In sum, Du Bois's disposition was toward the formal cultivation of paths to self-governance across the continent. After the First World War, Du Bois thought that the project of mandates and commissions of protection or trusteeship, particularly around the disposition of those countries held as colonies by Germany previous to the war, could yield such a favorable outcome. It did not. For Du Bois, the failure to address fully the matter of colonies in the agreements of Versailles in 1919 had left a prime basis for the eventual resumption of hostility among European nations. Thus, Du Bois, likewise thought that consideration of the status of European colonies in general, notably on the African continent, ought be addressed as a key aspect of the terms of peace and the postwar order as the Second World War came to an end, with the Allied victory. As Du Bois tells us in this 1945 essay, the formal and organizational movement of pan-Africanism, apart from any other conflicts or contradictions or failures of vision, foundered on the internal differences (at once political and theoretical) of policy on the future status of the relation of Africa (both as a putative whole and as the apparition of individual states and projects) to capital, most specifically capital from Europe and America. Written before the conference itself, this essay maybe taken as Du Bois's articulation of a fundamental disposition: a concern to thematize the whole problem of an autochthonous basis for relatively local forms of accumulation, in relation to world economic institutions and processes imbricated decisively with the whole history of systems of accumulation and capitalization that was rooted in enslavement and imperial colonization across the modern epoch. The epochal order of understanding may be understood as the pivotal aspect of Du Bois's thought of the historic project of a movement of pan-Africanism.

In April 1947, at a conference organized by Rayford W. Logan and held at Howard University in Washington, DC—the proceedings of which were later published under the heading "Trust and Non-self-governing Territories"—in a paper with the title "A Program of Emancipation for Colonial Peoples," W. E. B. Du Bois offered a presentation that amounted to a summation of the whole of that epochal theoretical disposition (Du Bois 1982e). On the occasion of that essay—just over three months following the publication of *The World and Africa*—while the frame is clearly global and taking as its definitive projection a concern to speak to the status of "colonized peoples," throughout the world, its principal coordinates were the worldwide and planetary terms of reference that he had formulated and elaborated over nearly six decades, from the last decade of the 1890s to the whole of the 1940s. These coordinates he had gathered and put forth as the frame for that book, writing across the whole of the years of 1945 and 1946. Just a year and a half earlier, writing in his newspaper column, "As the Crow Flies," in the *Amsterdam News* in August of 1944, Du Bois had identified the project of which all of this writing and thinking was an expression. It was focused on the matter to which he would devote himself "for the remaining years of [his] life," as he saw it at that time.

> The greatest question before the world today is this: can we have Democracy in America and Europe so long as the majority of the peoples of the world are in colonial status; kept poor and ignorant and diseased for the profit of the civilized nations of the world? This is the problem to which I propose to devote the remaining years of my active life. (Du Bois 1986)

Du Bois formulates this question along two theoretical lines in his 1947 presentation, each of which has to do with understanding—in a broad sense being able to do something, to produce something, or bring something about, as the essential condition of action, especially for any collective or in the context any form of sharing or being at stake together—as the primary constitutive condition of action. The two lines of problem of understanding that ought to become of theoretical concern are, respectively, knowledge (an epistemological matter) and representation (a political and economic matter).

I offer a brief elaboration of these two lines in terms of three formulations. They are simple, yet profound.

In the first formulation of his essay, of a historiographical perspective on the part of Du Bois, he understood colonies in the twentieth century as an expression of the historicity of the modern epoch as a whole. They are its tendentious expression on a planetary scale of reference, at the time of Du Bois's writing, modern colonies the world over, "those people who in one way or another have come under the ownership and control of Europe for 550 years," and thereby have "been used to bolster and advance the progress of Europe" (Du Bois 1982e 228).

In the second formulation, of politics and economics, Du Bois annotates that as an expression of an historical projection of democracy, colonies ought to have the production of their own well-being as their guiding ideal (and not in any fundamental sense the well-being of others as their purpose). Likewise, as corollary, Du Bois proposes that the same guiding idea ought stand for the working classes of Europe and America, in general, but especially so for all "colored" or African American folk.

The third formulation might be understood as directly a matter of theory. In Du Bois's critical and theoretical judgment, the means to produce democracy on a worldwide scale, by way of taking "colonial peoples" as the primary terms of reference, is to reorient their relation to capital. Apart from any immediate gesture to inscribe such thought within the frame of a Marxism of any kind, Du Bois's conception here ought be referenced first to a premise of equity as an expression of a commitment to self-determination and a form of social constitution that would be democratic in that from which it takes resource and that toward which it would grant its intention. The historicity of an African American practice of making a way out of no way is affirmed herein, in this dimension of Du Bois's thought of the historial, such as it is expressed in his declaration toward the productions of the African American spiritual. Such would be behind a general recognition of possibility that we might affirm with Du Bois, among and from the once "colonized" peoples. Further then, whatever one might say of primary capital (or a "primitive accumulation") and capitalization in general, or such principle as the telic definition of any accumulation, Du Bois in this essay works the thought that in principle one might move away from the idea of expropriation in general, or extraction (of all sorts), as a telic moment in any productive practice, and toward the idea of sustainable reproduction—with the matter of the removal of labor from any principle of commodification and to understand it instead as the constitutive element in any new conception of "capital." In this essay, Du Bois may be understood to begin with a conception of labor as otherwise than a commodity—certainly with reference to other forms of production, given across the historical past other than capitalist practices, but oriented toward the conceptualization of futural such forms—according to an understanding of economy, even a political economy, as otherwise than grounded in a distinction of labor vis-à-vis capital.

We can remark this thought first in terms of historicity in the past within the modern epoch. A key reference is a theoretical understanding of the status of enslavement in the modern context, of the Atlantic basin, in general. If enslaved labor can be mortgaged and thus translated into "capital" (perhaps a so-called liquid form of such, whereby it may be further translated, or even converted into another mode of currency as value), that we may remark according to its dominant idioms of articulation, social and economic, and political, for example. Then, such enslaved labor can be conceptualized as a form not radically or categorically distinct from "capital," if thought according to a general understanding of economy. (We recall here, that Thomas Jefferson—only one example among others—used persons enslaved under his name as collateral for a large foreign loan from a Dutch banking house in order to finance the construction of Monticello [Wiencek 2012]). Such thought becomes possible in the epistemic space of Du Bois's critique of colonial accumulation; yet, likewise, it becomes a legible theoretical problematic in light of the historicity of modern systems of enslavement in the Americas. Thus, we may recall an earlier notation in this text (above) that with capitalism capital itself is not indifferent to so-called natural or historically construed differences of labor (or rather, such differences are always articulated therein). We may annotate the matter further here: capital seeks to make such differences useful and profitable. To pose the metaphor, here for the elucidation of concept, exploitation is always and everywhere by way of diacritical mark, by the general social deployment of the mark that give under the heading of the concept-metaphor of the colors of labor power. This is so as to remark the material specificity of the organization of labor as a specific and historical process. Such is tendentiously planet-wide or putatively global, as it were. "Capitalism," as an historical system always, without exception, takes over and sustains such supposed differences from the historicity of other modes of production (often too easily supposed as different on a categorical basis) and the diverse attendant social systems and makes possible the reinscription of such marks as diacritical indications within its "own" horizon of economy and value. In this way the whole complex may be understood as something quite other than an anachronism. Rather, it is the most contemporary, indeed fashionable, expression of the historicity of capital, itself always and everywhere always historical in its forms of existence. To account for this operation within the system of capitalist production, supposed natural differences ought be understood as an articulate mark that always and ineluctably re-marks labor, colorful, as the colors of labor power, as both constitutive condition and realizable effect (or rearticulates the marks of labor as a certain "colored" labor), which on the order of generations, shall we name it, may be analytically understood by (critical) measure as accumulation. A social being, for example, as supposedly "white," as in the case of Thomas Jefferson, is the being of one who can "own," in the form of an accumulated status and semiotic currency—which can manifest in quite diverse forms, for example, military, theological, etc. Whereas, with regard to "white laborers" of the Reconstruction era, Du Bois remarked it as a form of supplementary "psychological wage," the thought can be rendered general to name the whole sense of an accumulated social and historical status that can be tendentiously construed as "whiteness" over time, on the order of a telos of capitalization, exhibited, for example, in familial wealth, social and political standing, and the organization of resource. In Du Bois's conceptualization it is "a sort of public and psychological wage" that "the white group of labourers, while they received a low wage were compensated in part by a sort of public and psychological wage" (Du Bois 1976a: 700–1; Du Bois 1935). We may elaborate, and thus amplify, the theoretical implication over historical time, the "wage" tendentiously operates according to the telos of accumulation as capitalization. This might be the touchstone aspect of the economic meaning, for a general social and historical economy, of a thought of the colors of labor power, that we have begun to adumbrate here, as a path of theoretical consideration.

In like manner, we might now theoretically consider Du Bois's thought of the problem of the color line, now under the heading of possibility rather than limit, as the putatively "cultural" meaning—in general, that is to say as an index of *istoria* or the *historial*—of the thought of the colors of labor power.

That is to say that what must now be clarified is something of how Du Bois understood this question. The theoretical principle of his thought here is that there is in the modern dispensation, as *istoria*, a whole other way to understand resource and the possibility of another world, that is yet in this world, as the forms of the world or worlds that have not yet found passage, but may yet find a way, by way of colored folks (a general rather than a parochial reference)—those otherwise issuing in the articulations of the modern epoch by colonization or colonialism in general—as both condition and realization of such world, or worlds, that remain yet to come. This disposition is an expression of the whole of his comprehension of the history of the modern epoch as he had cultivated it, by way of his effort to become commensurate in thought with the problematization given in matters African American, matters African, and the historicity of modern enslavement and its aftermath, most especially the generative and originary historial production among and across the African Diaspora, throughout the Americas and the Caribbean. His formulation is not in any way an abandonment or a setting aside of the priority of his perennial concern. Rather, certainly, we can say rather directly, to place here the metaphor, matters are interwoven. However, even more, it is a fulsome articulation and expression of the way in which for Du Bois, the matter of Africa, shall we say, is indeed of the whole of the world. Yet, there is still more to this conception and formulation by Du Bois: the status of the "colonized," of the "colored folk" of the world is through and through in reciprocal condition to the "workers" of Europe and America. And, more radical still, as he had put it in an essay published in December 1944, as he completed the text of *Color and Democracy* and then would shortly begin work on *The World and Africa*, Du Bois staked the generalization: "democracy in America may continue to impede and nullify democracy in Asia and Africa" (Du Bois 1982a, 228). In thetic terms, such thought is simply a contrapuntal register of a primary critical thesis that Du Bois put forth in *Color and Democracy*, with regard to the promulgation of both World I and World War II: that the failure to realize democracy within the supposed colonial domain would portend the resurgence of disaster, in war, for any and all nations in Europe and the Americas that might proclaim themselves as a democracy. May we name this a theoretical chiasmus?

Still more, we can also recognize the theoretical emergence of the terms of an entirely other order of reference, the articulation of Africa as the name for a horizon of possibility beyond any and all such forms of historical limit.

In this light, we may summarize here Du Bois's "program for the emancipation of colonial peoples" as the afterthought of the itinerary of the books *Color and Democracy* (written during the closing three months of 1944) and *The World and Africa* (begun in concept in early 1945 and completed in writing at the onset end of the summer of 1946), as he declared it in the spring of 1947.

With regard to knowledge of the contemporary world historical situation in which the question of the colonies might be addressed, at mid-twentieth century, in the aftermath of the second of two World Wars within two generations, Du Bois gives two reciprocal historical indices: "modern western European civilization has collapsed" (260); that which "brought about the collapse of Europe in the thirties and forties of this century [the twentieth] were already the curse of colonial distress and made colonial peoples double victims of the modern age of capitalism," that is to say that for some five and a half centuries, as I noted above (Du Bois 1982e, 260). This has been done regardless of the "cost" to the colonized. The policies that produced this outcome were subordinated to quite simple, restricted, or limited and unsustainable, as well as brazen ideals: supposed self-regulating world markets; the economic organization of labor as a commodity; along with the organization of land as private property; and, the practical conception of "money as gold" (Du Bois 1982e, 260).

In like manner, Du Bois, conceived a doubled change in political and economic "representation," that the project of an order that would affirm worthy historical subjects, forms of human collectives of persons in common with dignity, as it were. Just as in Europe and America production ought to be for use and "distribution according to need" as the "ideal." Just so in the colonies, production ought to be for the benefit of the colonized, not "foreign profit." The baseline premise of this idea was "racial equality," that is to say, a sense of the human as common, not only general but as a universal shared sense of being. The "educated native ought not to be understood as an unusual phenomenon." More precisely, so too, the working classes of Europe and American might be uplifted on the terms of an idea of general value and possibility (Du Bois 1982e, 261–62).

Thus, if the sense of labor as other than commodity stands as a premise, then in principle and by way of a practical theoretical disposition, another horizon of value could open, to use contemporary and by future forms of knowledge (1) to "restore the ancient, cultural economy, with its family," but by way of a reference to knowledge as science (not as an archaism); (2) to "control work and wealth," as "modified by "modern knowledge"; (3) to plan and cultivate general public education, by way of government administration, without cost if possible, such that the ordinary person, of the masses, might "know what science has learned in the last two centuries" ("while the colonial peoples have been suppressed"); (4) to promote well-being of body and environs, so as "to restore the health and vitality of the former magnificent physique of primitive peoples"; and, finally, (5) to elaborate "self-rule," on a twofold base, the "abolition of segregation," and the formal provision for "self-rule" of "home markets" (most precisely and especially in all aspects of its imbrication with iterations of any forms of world market). The presumption guiding this elaboration of Du Bois's thesis was that "imperial colonialism is identical with the problem of poverty in Western Europe and America." The solution was the same for each: "democracy in politics and industry" (Du Bois 1982e, 262–64).

The premise, both as ground and theoretical elaboration, is that human existence, as life, is not "automatic" to bios as a way of being. Rather, it is given by way of judgment, sometimes determined, by a practical sense of purpose. In the future, henceforth from the time of the denouement of the Second World War, for the future, Du Bois thought that the determination of the values that might yield the terms of self-determination should be the program for "colonial peoples," that is the vast majorities of the peoples of the whole the earth.

Abreast the second decade of the twenty-first century, we may understand it, in light of his thought of a new and novel Africa, which is yet to come, as the rearticulation of the global problem of the color line, henceforth, now under the heading of possibilities that are yet to come, in general, and without given end.

Annotation IV

As we gesture toward the denouement of our brief reflection, it may be apposite to recall that the threshold political-epistemological disposition of *Color and Democracy*, completed across the time line of the last month of the year 1944 and the first month of the year 1945, is that twentieth-century European fascisms, which led to the promulgation of the Second World War, within a generation, were dimensions or expressions of a generalized, tendentiously global, epochal, promulgation of the suppositions of a deter- minate understanding of categorical differences among the supposed human, pertaining, that is to say, to the whole of modern historicity—entailing the entire itinerary of his engagement in thought. We can only begin to explain that problematization (whomever is such, this *we*) by way of reference to a generalized practical-theoretical conception of the problem of the color line, as Du Bois had begun to develop such a thought at the turn from the nineteenth to the twentieth century.

As we have noted above and continue to annotate here, the exemplary domains of such general, global, and epochal problematization are the his- tory of modern colonialism, and then (more deeply set still, constitutively) the history of modern systems of enslavement. In the context of our text, *Color and Democracy* Du Bois's deployment of this disposition animates a prophetic claim that the problem of the color line will in the future cause war, bring recurring tragedy, to humankind in general, and on a global scale of reference (Du Bois 1975a; Du Bois 1945).

Yet, there is also in this text the subtle expression of an abiding sense of hope—even if it is as an "unhopeful hope," in a sense that he had once described matters of the African American, in the opening chapter of *The Souls of Black Folk*. "Unhopeful hope," is a phrase by which Du Bois remarks the unstated form of the question of the future throughout this text; and then across the whole remainder of his itinerary. That is to say the commitment to "make a way out of no way," in a somewhat immemorial discourse of the African American traditions, is the guiding value of the articulation of the writerly voice of this late text. That is also to say that amidst the radical sense of horror, of the whole of the world at war, Du Bois calls forth a resonance from the historical (of the events of living) and historial (of the values addressing living as at once life and death) imagination, a lived sense of possibility as at once tactile and real, on the one hand, and yet also of an order of a the fantastic, on the other. For what concerns him here is at once an existential reality of the here and the now, that is nonetheless also beyond any form of mundane ambivalence—of sharing and hunger, of fear in pain as suffering and the joy of dance. This is to say further that while the sense of what is at stake for Du Bois in this text is certainly encoded in, or as, all of those existential and historical markers, his disposition also maintains an affirmation of the capacity to give that is otherwise than with regard to an economy of loss; indeed it is otherwise than economy in general. In all senses, this book might best be understood as a rather stern articulation of a near octogenarian's sense of an unhopeful hope held forth for the future youth of the world. The fantastic may also be understood as a constitutive thought and practice for Du Bois.

It is Du Bois's references to the domain of music that provide the rhetorical emplacement of hope within the text that is *Color and Democracy*.

It is his brief, for all appearances oblique but quite articulately staged, citations to music that make it possible for his text to become a declaration of unhopeful hope that yet remains radical in implication. His text issues at a moment of the most profound crisis of morals and belief on a planetary scale of reference. It issues astride the most devastating of wars—not simply of the century, or of his already fulsome existential lifetime of more than seven decades—but of the most global modern sense of historicity, of a lived sense of an epoch, if you will. (Du Bois's life course unfolded in birth in the immediate wake of one world historical war, the American Civil War, found its way beyond another, the First World War—during the time of which he suffered an illness that took him near death for months—a war that had already named for him, as for so many others, the unthinkable, even before his illness.)

Yet, within his text, his references to music are solicitations of a radical sense.

They are a solicitation of the past in the name of an unhopeful, yet hoped for, future.

It is perhaps distinctly notable that Du Bois, the major African American intellectual of the time, turns to quote, as he puts it at the end of chapter four of *Color and Democracy*, "two great Germans," of the long eighteenth century—Friedrich Schiller and Ludwig van Beethoven—by way of citations to a key passage of the fourth movement of the composer's ninth symphony (Du Bois 1975a, 99; Du Bois 1945). We recall here our early note that Du Bois's text is a book the preface to which was dated as signed on the first day of the first month of that fateful year of 1945. Yet, too, it is also notable, that Du Bois cites to the nineteenth century, to Richard Wagner's *Lohengrin* at the beginning of this text, at the end of its opening chapter (an opera that he had also cited in the penultimate chapter of *The Souls of Black Folk: Essays and Sketches* of 1903) and then to the African American spiritual, "Go Down Moses" at the close of the last chapter of his book (chapter 7) (Du Bois 1975a, 16, 143; Du Bois 1945). While Du Bois also quotes poetry throughout his discourse and affirms the seal of religious values as a potential means to solicit and bring to broad appeal (even as he notes his perennial hesitation and ambivalence toward organized religious practice, not so much toward its values as such) to a radical sense of the human, that he would ultimately seek to affirm, it is by way of the imagination of the future given as the music that he indexes in his text, above all, that Du Bois stakes both his affirmation and ongoing or renewed sense of hope.

As in the chapter epigraphs of *The Souls of Black Folk* issued at the opening of the century, Du Bois's major citations to music in this mid-century text, produce doubled references to music that is always of at least two different traditions (and, of course, never only two or double) (Du Bois 1903). This multiply refracting double indexing may be taken as the first principle of his citations. For, at its root, such double reference bespeaks, indeed exemplifies in rhetorical form, the theoretical premise of Du Bois's entire book—an affirmation of multiplicity and heterogeneity, diversity, as both genesis and telos, of the future as one of historial possibility.

Through the practice of a doubled musical allegoresis, configured at once, or simultaneously, through his references, Du Bois's citations configure an *anagogical* declaration. On the one hand, he cites to a supposed European tradition (notably German or Germanic tradition, of supposed high or elevated art). On the other hand, he specifies an example, theoretically understood, as in the title of his book, from among traditions of supposed "colored" folk (notably African American, of a supposed common or popular art).

That declaration, in turn, also stands as both a riposte and solicitation (as challenge) to the world, as the whole of the earth arrives on the threshold

of the momentous year of 1945. His declaration with regard to a supposed
Europe would be a gesture toward a traditionalized reference therein that
would be other than that historical figure's promulgation (as a certain Europe
or a certain America) of a fascist premise across the previous decade and a
half. Likewise, that declaration poses a thought of the capacity for a putatively
universal authority to find its genesis by active proposition from among the
folk that one might remark as "colored" across the scenography configured
on a planetary-wide basis at the approach to the mid-twentieth century.
There is a whole other—even if always and ineluctable in its apparition as
the same—historicity of the making of the world, not only of past or future,
but most precisely of the past in the future, that remains yet to come. It
promises a potentially originary practice of allegoresis, at once of value or
ideals (in Du Bois's language) and narrative or story (Jameson 2019). It is,
for Du Bois in these texts of the 1940s, an articulation that is always at
least and never only doubled in both its emergence and its duration, each
and respectively, that is also to say, also respectively, at once as practice and
as thought, a practical theoretical operation.

    At the inception of his text, the end of its first chapter, Du Bois refers
to Richard Wagner's opera *Lohengrin*, written during the years immediately
preceding the 1848 revolutions throughout Europe, and then first brought
to performance in 1850. Wagner's conception was developed from the
legend of a grail (as in the Arthurian legends) from the domains of what
is now understood as Northern and Western Europe—the account of a
divine dispensation manifested within the domains of this world (often in
the form of an object such as a platter, a cup, a chalice, or a stone)—as
that legend emerged within a narrative ensemble that began to issue forth
from the eleventh century of the common era. Du Bois's reference proceeds
by way of Wagner's construction of the fictional elaboration of the story of
the knight Lohengrin as it was developed out of a motif of the mythical
story of his fictional father, Parsifal. Although not the only source, Wagner's
telling was cultivated notably as this story complex was indicated in Wolfram
von Eschenbach's *Parzival* (Eschenbach 1980). (The latter, for example, is
dated to the first quarter of the thirteenth century, in the apparition of the
German telling—in tandem with the aftermath of assemblages of its nascent
emergence in the context of languages that we today think of as Gaelic and
French; it came to written articulation a century prior to the appearance of
Dante Alighieri's *Commedia* across the first quarter of the fourteenth century
[Dante 1999 (ca. 1320)].) In all the modes of its extended retelling across
the centuries, the story is an account of the status of the divine within

existence, the meaning of life, and the accrual of wisdom that provides a bequest and understanding of the true purpose of living. It is an account of an awakening of character or, supposed, spirit. Within the opera, the fate of a falsely accused "maiden," Elsa of Brabant, is restored to justice, by the knight Lohengrin, although disguised, who has come from the land of the Grail. It is a touchstone story within the historicity that has become known as Europe, a story of the joining of the natural and the supernatural.

Already in the telling of the apocryphal story "Of the Coming of John," which comprises the penultimate chapter of Du Bois's *The Souls of Black Folk*, issued in 1903, a citation to the opera Lohengrin is placed as one of the primary touchstones of the narrative (Du Bois 1903, 228–49). In the short story, the narrator has John Jones, a young, very recent, college graduate from the American South, stumble himself (so to speak) into a performance of Wagner's opera, *Lohengrin*, at New York's Metropolitan Opera House in Manhattan (located then at Broadway and Thirty-ninth), where under the sound of the opening music that accompanies the scene of the arrival of Lohengrin from across the waters by way of the famous "swan," John is lead to muse on the question of his true purpose in life.

Later in the narrative, after John's return to his hometown, in the wake of the utter failure there of his proffered enlightened oratory (perhaps claiming some version of "liberty, equality, and fraternity") from the pulpit of the local church to the his natal community in special assembly to hear him, and then too after the abrupt forced closure of the school that he had refounded for African American children, by action of the dominant white political figure in the town (known in the story as "the Judge"), John takes a radical action. He moves to protect his young sister Jennie, against the threat of sexual violation by his twinned "white" counterpart (who was his grade school playmate, and also a recent college graduate, like him, who was also named John, and son of the "Judge"). In the act, he kills this twinned John. From there, in the aftermath of this disaster, in his mind's-eye-memory, he recalls the drama of the moral imperative that solicits Elsa as a mortal by the calling given to her (and the Brabant community) by divine example, as staged in the opera *Lohengrin*.

John must remain true to what fate has given him, even as that gift yields for him disaster. Thus, in the penultimate paragraph of the short story, before a last strophe, the narrator apparently misquotes the key locution given to the heroine of the opera at the beginning of its third act (the famous bridal song) by the assembled "people" (of "Brabant," of the world of the opera). The phrase that appears in Wagner's libretto in the opening to the third act is "Treulich geführt ziehet dahin" (Guided by faith, go there [into the marriage bond given to you, Elsa, by Lohengrin]) (Wagner 1993 [ca. 1848]). Instead of the word *treulich*, which I render here as "with faith" (or with more literal sense, as "faithful"), the narrator in the story gives the key word of the supposed quotation in John's mind of the word from the opera in German as *freudig*. In turn, I render *freudig* here as "with joy," or in a more literal sense as "joyful." With this change to the libretto, as it is given to us by the narrator in the short story, as it is understood to occur in the mind of John, the character of the emotion shifts such that in his mind's-eye-memory, in his final hour, the phrase becomes, as "Freudig geführt ziehet dahin," it becomes at once imperative and declarative in its sense, for it may be translated as "joyful" (joyful [in being there/here, in being led there/here]). For, in all senses, for John, as character, for the narrator of his story, and for Du Bois as writer in performance, this displaced quotation (for it is something other than a simple misquotation) should be taken as a statement of understanding of the divine, even if mortal, fate, or purpose, or meaning made available to John's character. The quotation, performatively displaced, is now articulated within a new locutionary context, John's own locution, given within the narrative of his story—it is thus also performatively re-placed, if you will—within this new version of an apocryphal story, that some might now consider as also archetypal, now, that is, as the story of a Georgia boy of the American South at the turn to the twentieth century, not so much the story of the mythical world of Elsa of Brabant and the knight Lohengrin of the land of the grail, of the eleventh century of the common era (Du Bois 1903, 249, chap. 13, para. 54). Perhaps never again may the story of Lohengrin may be understood by the thoughtful without an indexical consideration of the story of John Jones, at the approach to the twentieth century.

In Du Bois's turn-of-the-century text of 1903, the citation of the Wagner opera functions as a double allegory. In the manner that Du Bois cites to the opera in his text *Color and Democracy* at the turn to the year 1945, such function is all the more precisely given; it is performative—indeed, it is emphatic in its textual performance.

In the mid-twentieth century text, Du Bois's citation is to the final and culminating scene of the third act, to the moment of the famous so-called grail narration, given in response by Lohengrin to the heroine, Elsa, who poses to him (now her husband), the one question that she is forbidden to ask of him: from whence does he come?

In the second scene of the opening act to the whole opera Lohengrin had declared to Elsa that she must not ask him one question. Elsa had promised in the affirmative. As the basis for his defense of her honor and their subsequent matrimony, he had asked of her: "musst Eines du geloben mir: / Nie sollst du mich befragen, / noch Wissens Sorge tragen, / woher ich kam der Fahrt, / noch wie mein Nam und Art!" ("you must promise me one thing: / never shall you ask of me, / nor trouble yourself to care to know, / whence I journeyed, / what is my name, or what is my kind!") (translation mine) (Wagner 1993 [ca. 1848]).

Of course, the turning point of our story is that eventually she does indeed ask the forbidden question.

Thus, in the final and culminating scene of the third act, as the famous narration, Lohengrin is compelled to confess his origin as supernatural, from the land of the grail—known in the opera as "Mount Salvat." The consequence of this revelation is that he can no longer remain as her husband, as mortal, as human. Rather, he must return to the land from whence he came, in another world, a supernatural world, as immortal, that is, as a "knight," a guardian, of the sacred. Du Bois describes this moment as the instance of Lohengrin's "disaster," remarking notably the music of this occurrence, within the opera, that is "the thrilling melody of Lohengrin's swan above his disaster." It is to the music of this scene (something more than just an aria), which is of the same sonic and orchestral character as the music of Lohengrin's entry into the opera-story, the scene that Du Bois had referenced in his 1903 short story, as well as the music of the famous prelude to the whole opera, which is associated with his character throughout the opera that Du Bois refers at the end of the first chapter of *Color and Democracy*.

Lohengrin's narration of his origins begins with phrase "In fernem Land, unnahbar euren Schritten. . . ." Although normally translated into English close to the literal as "in a far-off land, inaccessible to your steps . . . ," in the context of Du Bois citation to it at the inception of 1945, Lohengrin's reference to his origin would be more fulsomely understood as "in a foreign land . . . ," giving the sense not only of his genesis in the otherworld that is divine or supernatural and thus "inaccessible" to Elsa's mortal steps, but also to a sense of his natal origination as not native to the present context, foreign, if you will, foreign to the land and world of his wife (Elsa of Brabant) in the opera. He is from another land; he is foreign-born (Wagner 1993 [ca. 1848]).

The "disaster" in question may be understood in relation to the coming to naught of his most deep seated and fundamental mission. The breaking of the matrimonial bond means that the perpetual peace that his presence would provide must likewise be broken. In his own text, as his own political *poiesis*, Du Bois proclaims an allegorical bearing, notably ecclesiastical rather than celestial, for this dramatic course of events in the opera. Within the opera, the central leitmotif of the entire work is given its most fulsome expression here. This is the music of Lohengrin's disaster to which Du Bois takes reference, at the end of the first chapter of *Color and Democracy* (Du Bois 1975a, 16; Du Bois 1945).

According to his reference to that *music*, Du Bois would situate the historial status on a world-historical scale of reference for the eventuality of the historical Dumbarton Oaks conference, and all manner of diplomacy, in the general sense, that followed in its wake. Taking his incipit by a remark of the historic example of ancient Egypt, including the itinerary of historic Kush within that historicity, as the joining of the upper and lower Nile (a reference annotated further in his subsequent text *The World and Africa*, issued two years later, in 1947), notably annotating the principle of governance of heterogeneous lineage informing the pivotal later Kushite leader Taharqa), only then does Du Bois bring the matter to annotate the genealogy of a putative federalism on a world-historical scale that would be typically annexed in Europe and America to its own claim to *historial* leadership. Du Bois as usual in his thought, indexes the historical Mediterranean—emphasizing what he calls in *Darkwater* "of the 'dago' Mediterranean shore"—in a manner constitutively distinct from the dominant narrative lines that privilege a certain idea of Europe. He proceeds otherwise than according to the then dominant narratives of Europe's and America's making and its dominant ideas of a "worldwide" confederation of nations and states. Those dominant stories try to maintain such a limited and parochial appurtenance down even to the mid-twentieth century, the historical configurations that followed one apocalypse (that of World War I), while yet astride another (that of World War II), the latter whose major volcano was yet to give its most fulsome eruption, across 1945 (Du Bois 1976d: 98–115, 201–25; Du Bois 1947; Du Bois 1975b: 40; Du Bois 1921; Pope 2014). Du Bois distinctly produces another set of narrative references, down to the time of his writing.

> The Double Crown of Egypt, the Achaean League, the Empire of Rome and the Holy Roman Empire, the Holy Alliance and the League of Nations, all listened to that high and striving chord of human unity above the discord of hate, hurt, and pain-like the thrilling melody of Lohengrin's swan above his disaster." (Du Bois 1975a, 16; Du Bois 1945)

Du Bois was writing approximately half a year before the advent of the conference, in which he participated as a delegate representing the NAACP, from the end of April 1945 to the end of June 1945, that would eventuate in the formation of the United Nations. Likewise, in recollection, we annotate such matters here, for I write these words as we cross the time line of the seventy-fifth anniversary of that founding. We must, therefore also, most assiduously recall, that the two deployments of nuclear weapons in war unfolded in the interregnum, August of 1945, before that founding conference of a new united League of Nations was ratified by the world community of nations, in October, the autumn of that year (for which Du Bois gave testimony before the US Senate Committee on Foreign Relations (Du Bois 1980). Thus, too, we remark in apposition that Barack Hussein Obama became the first US head of state to visit a site of that deployment, at Hiroshima, Japan, in memorial, while holding office (Obama 2016).

To encourage a theoretical recognition of the place of music in Du Bois's thought in this text, we can underscore the performative dimension at stake here. As already noted, the sound of the music of the grail "narration" of the third act (the moment of "disaster") was associated with the character of Lohengrin throughout the opera. In fact, in a biographical and historical sense, it was the first music composed by Wagner for the whole opera. Thus, it came to stand as the monogram for the opera as a whole. Later, it gave its signature to the famous prelude, which was written last by Wagner and to the almost equally famous opening scene of the knight's arrival, in the worldly domain of "Brabant" in the opera—from over the waters drawn by the "swan"—to the defense of the falsely accused maiden, Elsa. Indeed, such association, of character and sonic strophe, if you will, became a signature for the new music of Richard Wagner as a whole, thereafter, eventually, definitive, throughout his musical itinerary. As I noted above, in his 1903 citation to this opera in the story of John Jones, "Of the Coming of John," it was the music of the scene of Lohengrin's arrival (of the first act), that Du Bois first specifically referenced (Du Bois 1903, 235–38, chap. 13, paras. 12–15). For us, in our reading it may now thus be also said that the music of Lohengrin has become also the music of John Jones, of Altamaha, Georgia, according to the life of fiction, literature, and the telling of story in general. It is now also of John's own. That is to annotate, that nearly forty years apart, Du Bois indexed to the same music as given in two iterations, in two distinct scenes, in the drama of the opera, one from its opening, one from its closing. In each case Du Bois notes the sonic and symbolic height, as in supposed transcendence, of the sound given as music. Despite the despair and foreboding that attends each scene, carried within the sonic dimensions of this music, which will yield to the tragic eventual outcome of its final scene (Lohengrin's departure and the worldly loss of the reassurance of the sacred dispensation that he bears into the world of the mortals), in which the heterogeneity of mortal and immortal is brought into relief by way of the insensible movement of the forbidden question, it is yet music, which in the torsion of the limit in its articulation (as *res extensa*, in the physical dimension that we know as sound), that which gives it as music, in all of its dimensions, nonetheless also opens the symbolic way to a measure of hope, perhaps indeed immeasurable. It may be understood to remark limit as also yet the threshold for another inhabitation of possibility.

Writing at the turn to that fateful year, 1945, of the second worldwide calamity of war, within a generation, Du Bois claims this hope, in the face of ongoing, and yet also impending, disaster, as historical eventuality in his lived sense of world. The citation to *Lohengrin* thus produces a redoubled allegory. The citation may be understood in a rhetorical sense as the production of a *redoubled double* allegory. It is an allegoresis that goes all the way down and all the way up, at once.

In brief theoretical summary we might say that within the world of the opera, the supernatural (world of the grail) intervenes in the world of the natural (historical world, of Brabant), or worldly world. It is a mythical account of a higher authority (extra-ordinary) intervention in the mundane (ordinary). As mythical, its basis is an ideological affirmation of belief, or acknowledgment, on the part of a subject (as in subjective, of subjectification), which is at once semiotic, linguistic, and sonic. (This is to cite thus, yet annotate, the recent magisterial apostrophe of Frederic Jameson in this regard [Jameson 2019].) This is to say too, in a somewhat different register, that it is likewise, always, through and through, material (sometimes comprising *materiel*, in the military sense of the word), of extension, that is also, at once, temporal and spatial. Even more, the world of which it is an account (and the events therein, the story), take on the status of a symbol (semiotic and historical). The world of which it gives an account is symbolic. The telling, the account, is then the practice of an allegoresis. It stands as a supple, always resourceful, allegory of the de facto historical present (this latter in the nonsimple sense suggested above).

Within the worlds of the historicity of his own writing, by way of, as well as within, his writing, Du Bois takes that which might be accepted and affirmed, as Brabantian, a northern European mythical (allegory of) world and appropriates it for refraction on the de facto historical world, of the times of his writing. In the year 1903, it is the world of the American South—which we may also remark as worlds, in the plural—namely, config-ured in narrative around the character of John Jones and, his sister, Jennie Jones, a small town, of coastal Georgia, in the United States of America (Du Bois 1903d, 228–49, chap. 13).

In the context of Du Bois's short story "Of the Coming of John," in *The Souls of Black Folk*, on the one hand the opera itself and on its own stands in as mythical, from far away, while, on the other, the mythical opera world and the narratives of the historical northern European world may each (respectively) be understood with suitable tuning to stand as an otherworldly *allegorein* for a certain historiographical or historiological understanding of the world(s) of the Georgia coast of the post–Civil War American South (at the eastern end of a "Black Belt," as Du Bois wrote of it, that extended from northeastern Texas to the coast of the sea islands of the Carolinas, Georgia, and northern Florida) (Du Bois 1903d, 110–62, chaps. 7 and 8).

At January 1945, it is the world of the whole world, if you will, as played out in the massive aggression of the Second World War, as exemplified in the promulgation of all that was at stake in the German theater of war, and then so too the European theater in general, especially its northern, eastern, and western fronts.

Aside from the collective historical events of the war itself, there was also entailed for Du Bois an existential eventuality within this whole conjuncture.

As an existential referent for the deployment that I noted above of *Lohengrin* in the short story of John Jones in *The Souls of Black Folk* in 1903, it was in the 1890s (perhaps during the year 1893) as a twenty-something student abroad for the first time, for some two years of graduate study at Berlin, that Du Bois first experienced opera. Then, after intermittent visits during the intervening decades, in late 1935, Du Bois was successful in secur-ing a grant to spend a few weeks to study industry and educational policy in Germany. For August and September of 1936, while based in Berlin, he did not from all apparent indications attend the Olympic festivities. What gains our attention more than educational policy or international sport, is Du Bois's attention to music. He spent a full week at the famous Bayreuth Festival in Bavaria from August 19 to 25. On the first day of his visit at the festival, he attended the now infamous production of *Lohengrin*. Then, after a break of one day, he attended on subsequent days all four operas of Wagner's cycle *Der Ring Des Niebelungen*. (Among several other items from the Bayreuth Festival of August 1936 retained in the W. E. B. Du Bois Papers, one can note the ticket stubs for these performances.) A recent biography of Wagner indicates that in adoring attendance at the festival performance of *Lohengrin* was Adolf Hitler, while noting that Thomas Mann, in exile in Switzerland, also adoring, listened by radio, as the opera "was broadcast as part of the celebrations marking the one-thousandth anniversary of the founding of the German Reich" (Geck 2013, 301–2). Yet, too, on a broader level and in a more fundamental sense, we underscore that Wagner's music and the Bayreuth Festival were consistently presented by the Third Reich as its exemplum (Thurman 2012: 610). Du Bois's own inhabitation of the ensemble of conjunctures attendant to Wagner's work in relation to the Third Reich for some ten years at the time of his writing of *Color and Democracy* was direct, intense, and overdetermined. His decision to cite Wagner's text at the outset of his essay, as one may understand his writing here, was an emphatic statement of the capacity (as both a right and a willful claim, that is as an insistent declaration) of a reference to the opera, or an interpretation of it, stakes an eventual meaning of the opera that would be otherwise than any such understanding that might be completely subsumed to the historical Nazi appropriation of this work, during the 1930s and 1940s.

After emplacing a key scholastic notation, there are three temporal indices that we might lay across the brief historical reference that we have made to the interwar period and the duration of the Second World War. These notations may be useful for an ongoing future critical contextualization of the thought and art at stake as the politics of Du Bois's theoretical practice, as we have annotated it here.

As a scholastic matter, we note that among Du Bois's unpublished papers in the archive at the University of Massachusetts, there is a very brief handwritten note of an idea for a short story titled "The Secret Singer." It reads: "A black girl has a phenomenal voice. Rubinstein hears her. Rehearses her behind curtain & sells her to Klan Kleagle & Co. They plan her debut. She is black. The Ave Maria! Rubinstein hears applause. [Rubinstein] takes her back for friendship and hands off. [illegible] She succeeds as Aida" (Du Bois ca. 1920b). (Brackets above are mine. Perhaps the name given in that note indicates the great Polish-born, later American citizen, pianist Arthur Rubinstein, of Jewish family background and heritage, who first came to prominence in the US in the later teen years of the twentieth century.) Likewise, from the archive, we know by way of a handwritten letter of May 4, 1921, in careful script, from Marian Anderson to Du Bois, in a somewhat formal reply to an inquiry by him in an immediately previous letter that he had most likely already come to know of her musical brilliance and accomplishment (she was born in Philadelphia, in the same year as his lost, firstborn, a son, whom Du Bois had eulogized in *The Souls of Black Folk*). Then too, already from 1927, in her thirtieth year (she would live to the age of ninety-six), Anderson would leave her natal country of the United States to practice her art in Europe. Over the course of the decade thereafter she performed from the outset with ever-growing acclaim across the continent, including especially in Berlin, Salzburg, and Vienna, as well as working in collaboration with the Finnish composer Jean Sibelius (who also composed some songs directly for her), as well as a widely noted recognition by the legendary conductor Arturo Toscanini as indeed a voice "heard once in a hundred years" (Thurman 2019: 843).

With that scholastic annotation in place, we can place here our *first* contextual or historiographical mark with a notice of Anderson's artistic itinerary in central Europe amid the 1930s, specifically by the time that Du Bois arrived in Berlin in the summer of 1936. After a notable performance with the Vienna Philharmonic in June of 1936, the *Neues Wiener Journal* wrote: "It might surprise you that Marian Anderson comes to us primarily as an interpreter of German classical music; but whoever has once heard her sing Schubert, Schumann, or Brahms knows that her relationship with German musical art is utterly convincing." (daß sie zur deutschen Tonkunst in einem restlos überzeugenden Verhältnis steht.) Six months thereafter, from early in 1937, Anderson would begin and maintain a ten-month residency in Berlin itself (Thurman 2019: 842–47, as quoted at 846–47). Although "her linguistic mastery of the poetry and her musical mastery of the score made her a phenomenon," almost as a native, the decisive problematic remained. The remark of her articulation of such art with surprise, whether affirmative or negative, even to mention her apparition as without need of remark, encoded the fundamental philosophical and political theoretical *seme*: the unavowed, yet all the more decisive because unremarkable "assum[ption] that whatever was [B]lack could not also be universal and that what was universal could not be tainted by ethnic particularism, leaving whiteness untouched and unspoken" (Thurman 2019: 849, brackets mine).

With a recognition of the place of the new mass media, most especially the radio, in conjunction with the staging of massive public events by the Nazi regime, the 1936 Olympic games at Berlin were understood within that regime as primarily a world-historical occasion for its self-projection. Thus, our second mark of eventual historicity is given by the utterly unique announcement within this unprecedented media horizon: the athletic accomplishments of Jesse Owens. The son of a family imbricated by historical sharecropping (which Du Bois had described in the seventh and eighth chapters of *The Souls of Black Folk*, as the "Black Belt"), Owens won four gold medals, between August 3 and 9 at those games. Although he was the most successful of the athletes at those games, with his four gold medals remaining without equal for more than a generation, standing thus in marked articulation that by example contradicted the claims of the host regime, it was the relative absence of official affirmation of that accomplishment within the United States (national level sports organizations and the US government) that remains most notably also attendant to that success. His success was another African American example of excellence, across the Berlin and Europe of the time of Du Bois's arrival there in the summer of 1936.

As Du Bois wrote *Color and Democracy* in 1944, astride the last surges in the European theater of the Second World War, we may now understand his reference to art, music in general, *Lohengrin* as exemplar, to have been affirmed by the near transcendent exemplars of a possible African American—hence African, hence American, hence European, hence worldwide—*futural* possibility.

We then arrive at a third index of historical articulation, by way of reference to two subsequent eventualities in which African American practitioners rearticulated the historial sense, if you will, inscribed by Du Bois in his writing about Wagner's *Lohengrin*, both 1903 and 1945. The rearticulation concerns both the Bayreuth Festival and the opera *Lohengrin*, respectively.

On the one hand, we note that as part of an effort to move the Bayreuth Festival beyond the lingering cloud of its past association with the Third Reich, an effort that included a visual aggression on the traditional presentation of the festival, by the postwar use of minimalist, rather symbolic, modern production, in 1961 the opera director Wieland Wagner (grandson of the composer), selected an African American singer, Grace Bumbry, for her premier performance in the role of Venus in Wagner's opera *Tannhäuser*. The resonance of the response to that casting has continued, even into the second decade, on the cusp of a third, in the twenty-first century (Thurman 2012).

Of greater pertinence for the perspective on this historicity at stake here as that has been bequeathed to us by way of the itinerary in thought of Du Bois, we note the launch at the end of that decade, the 1960s, of the astonishing decades-long career of the late Jessye Norman, a soprano of almost unparalleled range, across the major opera houses of Europe, while based from the outset in Berlin. Fitting symbolic heir to the historic example of Anderson, we note as our touchstone for this third index, her recorded work, widely available, but specifically as included in the studio production of *Lohengrin* from September 1985 to June 1986, with her singing the role of Elsa, against the quite versatile tenor of Plácido Domingo (of Spanish, Mexican, and Argentinian background), and the Vienna Philharmonic, under the conductor Georg Solti (of Jewish, Hungarian, background) (Wagner 1987). That before the century in which Du Bois wrote was out, Elsa of Brabant would be performed and put to record under the voice of a singer of such accomplishment, exceptional far beyond even her generation (whose astonishing delivery of an aria, an excellence, was reputed to have once caused the Viennese-born conductor Herbert von Karajan to almost become distracted, as he was on stage next to her, conducting), Du Bois could hardly have anticipated. He certainly had not declared any such hope in 1903 when he wrote of Jennie Jones in "Of the Coming of John." Nor is it likely that he thought of Elsa of Brabant—given in performance by the person of a singer of African American provenance—as his once imaginary or putatively fictional "secret singer" of his circa 1920 notations (as noted above) emerged de facto in the form of the inimitable personage of Marian Anderson. Yet, even if we discover that it was not the first time, the historical configuration of a rather phantasmic thought of his imagination is precisely what was given in the musically impeccable inhabitation that Norman exemplified in her work within this opera astride the 1980s, as we annotate it in light of the practical-theoretical political rearticulation that Du Bois had proposed for it by his citation at the end of the first chapter of *Color and Democracy: Colonies and Peace* in January 1945. Yet, even more, we can now also say that already in Du Bois's own meditations at the turn to the twentieth century, the historicity of Georgia of the American South and the European symbolic world of the supposedly mythical and fabled past and contemporary northern Europe, even Germany, of the mid-twentieth century were fully at stake in his thinking *at once and in respective relation to each other*, one being at stake most precisely by way of the other, as in the practice of an allegoresis, that I propose we understand as a practice of *double* allegory.

I offer now two footnotes, if you will, as a close to this discourse toward a sense of future at the limit of world.

As the final lines of the pivotal fourth chapter of *Color and Democracy: Colonies and Peace*, titled "Democracy and Color," Du Bois refers to Ludwig van Beethoven's most famous work, his Symphony No. 9 in D Minor, Opus 125, of 1824, which reinscribed, with modification, Friedrich Schiller's 1885 poem "An die Freude," the Ode to Joy, in its fourth movement (Du Bois 1975a: 99; Du Bois 1945). Likewise, as in his citation to *Lohengrin*, this reference to the fourth movement of Beethoven's Ninth Symphony is an inscription directly poised against the appropriation—ongoing at the time of Du Bois's writing—of the art of this other "great German" by the Third Reich, for the purposes of its self-projection. It is decisive, however, that we briefly annotate the terms of this second citation. For, although composed nearly a quarter of a century after Beethoven's symphony, Wagner's opera posed a harkening to a divine intervention in the mundane affairs of mortals. Beethoven's symphony is positioned as a different order of solicitation. Poised on the cusp of a movement from a solicitation of the Divine (here I mark it in capital inscription), configured simultaneously according to the Hellenistic Elysium (a reference to the domain of the afterlife that antedates the Christian dispensation and doctrine) and yet also to the Protestant evocation of a celestial resonance ("above the starry skies"), the ultimate solicitation of the fourth movement of Beethoven's last symphonic work is to the human, here understood as "all men" or all humankind, "Alle Menschen."

Du Bois cites the following passage from the fourth movement. "Alle menschen— / Seid umschlungen, Millionen!" (Here, in written text only, I must allow this reference to the libretto to also refer us to the music—both to the linguistic, that is, as it is given in voice, as well as to the sonic in general, that is specifically as it is given with other instruments.) We can give the English translation in rather literal terms: "All men [or all humans, humankind]—you millions, I embrace [this embrace is for all, humans]." Let us place as mark here that this citation does not displace, not explicitly, a masculine emplacement of the pronouns that operates in Schiller's inscription of the poem. That operation is sustained in Beethoven's libretto. As each line of Du Bois's quotation of the libretto, is not of a continuous line, but rather is respectively from two different parts of its second stanza, it is apposite for us to take his citation as indicating the libretto as a whole, and then so too to the whole of the fourth movement, and then to entire symphony, in metonymic reference. He is citing to the music and cadence, notably including the human voice, of the central motivic development for the symphony as a whole that Beethoven discovered in composing the fourth movement.

Without remark here on the excessive, indeed rather inflationary, appropriation of this extraordinary music over the duration of the twentieth century and beyond, following the end of the Second World War—indeed we can note the European Union designation of it as the anthem for the union as a direct reinscription against the Nazi appropriation—here I wish to accent the problematic of its status as the question of the *futural* heterogeneity of its implication.

In the light of Du Bois's citation, it is a matter of a fidelity that is at once a perennial restitution of a commitment to finding a way, where there is no way, with the simultaneous practice of a willingness to affirm the discovery of a possible way that has as yet been the very name of the impossible, in the face of the unimaginable, that may be affirmed as the placing at stake for self, an avowal thereto: the radical heterogeneity in generosity—the capacity to give. With the work of Cecil Taylor in mind, we may remark such capacity as the masculine maternal, or the masculine feminine; or, that is perhaps also to say, of generosity, as a name for that from which all things begin, of hospitality. (This latter is here cited in an African American sense of that word, of all genders—but notably, as the historicity of our time—of woman as mother, which may yet also include therein that which may be understood as masculine.) It is to affirm the passive in generation (Chandler 2018). If this is so, may Du Bois's solicitation recall or affirm such a horizon, as both an articulation of the given, as yet, or thereby, as also illimitable?

It is to affirm the future as always more than a simple or a one.

I may be permitted reference here to two instances of the articulation of such possibility from the teen years of the twenty-first century.

The first instance is registered by the conductor Daniel Barenboim in the documentary of the tour by the West-Eastern Divan Orchestra founded by the conductor with the late scholar Edward Said, formed of young musicians from Palestine, Israel, various Arab countries, and Spain, performing all nine of Beethoven's symphonies, concluding with the Ninth presented in the DMZ (the demilitarized zone) between the North and the South on the Korean peninsula. In an interview, Barenboim tells the story of a conversation in which someone asked a member of the Kinshasa Symphony Orchestra, an African musician, "'Would it not be more to the point if you played your music rather than playing our Beethoven' to which this African musician says, 'What gives you the right to say 'our Beethoven'?'" (Barenboim and Waldman 2012, quotation at 38:00; Stew 2006).

The second query in the story that Barenboim shares may be taken less as a gesture toward a putative universalism than toward an affirmation of the ineluctable heterogeneity given in the emergence and articulation itself as the condition, the very possibility, of that emergence and the latter's perdurance, necessarily as something else—a possible impossible way—altogether.

The other, or second, instance is to the recording of a performance of Beethoven's symphony, Opus 125, by the Chicago Symphony Orchestra and Chorus on September 18, 2014. With the support of donors, a visual and sonic recording of that performance has been made freely available on the internet since the spring of 2015 through the Chicago Symphony Organization's multiple venues online, including their own (Beethoven 2014). It is apposite to note that in addition to the associate concertmaster and the assistant concertmaster, approximate to a dozen other members of the violin section, as well as additional members among members of other string instruments, are women of Asian background (of the USA, South Korea, China, Taiwan, Australia, and Japan, and perhaps other natal references), in addition to fronting several Asian men in key positions within the orchestra. This notation is perhaps to attune to the register of (cultivate) an insight, of second generation, Illinois native, Korean American, violinist (with a major international solo career), Jennifer Koh—noting that Beethoven's so-called Kreutzer Sonata, Opus 47, for violin, was in fact originally dedicated by the composer to his Polish-born friend, George Bridgetower, a violin virtuoso, whose genealogy included an immediate reference to Africa—that such historical eventualities, genealogies of symbolic practice and artistic production, that attend to the music may be understood to solicit, that is, to bring forth, as its future, a mark of heterogeneity within the composition, a mark the registration of which was in all truth a constitutive condition for its incipit. The apparent re-resonance of the tradition in which Beethoven's musical bequest is usually situated (as performed by the Chicago Symphony and its Chorus in September of 2014, or as recently performed by Koh, for example) is only by way of the *re-inauguration* of openness or being at stake, that is, its indelible incipit (all the way up and all the way down); that is to say, of its possible address—not to the past—but to the future that remains yet to come (Koh 2016, at 3:30–13:45).

Yet, too, we recognize in that recording by the Chicago Symphony Orchestra and Chorus the delivery of those pivotal words of the fourth movement of the symphony that were quoted by Du Bois in his 1945 text in the indelible voicing—sonic and linguistic, as well as specifically musical—of the Philadelphia-originated bass-baritone Eric Owens, of African American background: ". . . alle Menschen werden Brüder / wo dein sanfter Flügel weilt. . . . / Seid umschlungen, Millionen! / Diesen Kuß der ganzen Welt!" [. . . all men become brothers / where your gentle wing rests. . . . / Receive this embrace, you millions! / This kiss is for the whole world!]. Impeccably robust and dapper in visual stature, this presentation of an African American

singer, with consummate gravitas and a sonorous diction at once dramatic
and precise, was undoubtedly marked by the hand of the music director and
conductor Riccardo Muti, likewise too, the astonishing organization of that
orchestra's twenty-first-century string section (a directorial disposition already
exemplified in his two immediate predecessors, Barenboim and Georg Solti,
each noted above). Hence, although one can index Owens's 2014 performance
to a tradition of singers of the past who have presented these words in the
historic presentations of this symphony, notably of European (if not only
German) reference, another possible hearing is entirely legible for us here.
It is the sonic and emotional historicity of the African American spiritual,
and then too, to the legacies of the African American sermon. With that
index, an entire ensemble of undulating historical references rearticulate the
indications of Beethoven's symphony, even as it simultaneously maintains all
of those markings (sonic, visual, and linguistic) that are habitually recognized
as already set loose within more traditional settings of its presentation. A
few may be briefly noted: the search for renewed hope in the face of the
unimaginable, in this latter sense, that is, the reference to the experience
of capture and coercion of body and being (of a duration on the order of
centuries); of the declaration of lived truth, quite apart from any dominant
forms of sanction or acknowledgment; of the search for guidance, both existential and historial, as given or as encoded, for example, respectively, in a
spiritual, such as "My way is cloudy"; to the search for fugitive knowledge,
as exemplified in the status of the metaphor, in all of its reality, given in
the phrase, "the North Star"; to the cadences of a "dream," given at once
in the strophe of Phillis Wheatley of the eighteenth century, of W. E. B.
Du Bois writing at the end of the fifth chapter of *The Souls of Black Folk*,
just after the turn from the nineteenth century, or of Martin Luther King
Jr. in full oratory at the Great March on Washington astride the 1960s of
the twentieth century. For, from this tradition across the centuries, there
has too been a resolute embrace of the future—now an invocation on the
order of the billions, of human, kind.

     In this regard, for this singer, Eric Owens, without reduction of his
path to that of one who has gone before, doubtless, we may yet be allowed
to call forth one name to sustain these resonances here, in discourse and
dialogue—one of the closest of friends for Du Bois in the last stages of his
itinerary: Paul Robeson (Robeson 1991).

     Yet, further still, as the resolute end of his discourse, at the end of its
last chapter, Du Bois himself takes direct resource to this African American
tradition, of the enslaved and their progeny, as given in the tradition of

"spirituals" (or, "sorrow songs" as he had nominalized them in the last chapter of *The Souls of Black Folk*). He closes the 1945 text with citation to the name of the spiritual "Go Down Moses" (with an exclamation mark added to its title, making of it an imperative and a perhaps militant invocation as solicitation, "Go down Moses!") and a musical staff indicating a bar of notes, without words. And those words, although they are not indicated within his text, were yet known the world over, since the decade following the Civil War, by way of the worldwide tours of the Fisk Jubilee Singers—of which Du Bois was once a member (Fisk Jubilee Singers 1997). Those words too, indicated a reception and reinauguration, anew, of an ancient Jewish and Judaic premise (as encoded in the Hebrew tradition at Exodus 7:16), as of fundamental value and virtue, articulating within a historial practice, among the enslaved, otherwise long unavowed in public discourses in America across that century, or supposed as of a low tradition, respectively (Bible 1966). This reference takes us into the roots of modern historicity, ongoing, in a manner that we in turn can still resolutely affirm.

The citation of Du Bois to this tradition may doubtless be taken as reference to both (1) the performances of the Fisk Jubilee Singers of the three quarters of a century previous, to the time of his writing, as well as, (2) for example, Marian Anderson's emergence into an accomplishment without contemporary parallel among singers worldwide, over the previous two decades. Her stellar realization was indexed not only by her touchstone 1936 recording of that specific spiritual, but above all by her landmark 1939 performance at the Lincoln Memorial in Washington, DC, before an estimated crowd of 75,000, and a radio audience of several million. She presented music in such a way that she exhibited without claim her inhabitation of doubled traditions, if you will. She may be understood to have produced a diacritical remark of this inhabitation, for during the opening song of her performance, "America (My Country 'Tis of Thee)," she notably replaced the preposition "of" with the preposition "to" in the phrase "of America I sing," and made the singular as of a collective, third-person plural, "we": instead of "*of* thee *I* sing," she sang "*to* thee *we* sing." She may be understood to have deployed in a manner that we may theoretically understand as of the same disposition that Du Bois had formulated in the opening chapter of *The Souls of Black Folk* of 1903: the sense of matters African encoding a doubled reference and resource and tradition, which thereby is exorbitant to (exceeding from within) to any inclination to reference a supposed preter-natural and narrow idea of America, that one might understand apart from that which she (and Du Bois) claimed as African American—notably the tradition of the spirituals from those who for centuries had been enslaved within America (Anderson 1999 [1936]; Anderson 1939; Du Bois 1903d; Chandler 1993). The citation to the spiritual "Go Down Moses," by Du Bois in *Color and Democracy* may be understood to produce an indexical reference, whether or not it was his declared intention (known or unknowable), to the historicity that enfolds the eventuality remarked in the late 1930s itinerary of performance of the traditions of the African American spiritual by Marian Anderson.

Finally, it must be remarked, this song of the centuries was one of the first of the African American spirituals inscribed and published at the outset of the American Civil War. Yet its bearing was already inscribed, otherwise. It marks within the historicity of the modern epoch—at once American, European, and African, perhaps we are within rights to also speak here of the global—an originary articulate vision of hope, for the future, as an issue *from* all of those once understood to have arrived late, somehow, on the thresholds of historicity. Here it is encoded in black, to stake the metaphor. For the historicity encoded in these songs was something other than a dispensation of a moral leadership from above; rather, it was an emergent articulation from within and beneath, from among those once thought of as the damned, a visioning of another world, this one, here, now.

As our final mark or measure, then, I offer three notes. Taking the song "Go Down Moses" in its metonymic function, for Du Bois, we recall (as we now know) that famously it was likely known by him as a touchstone song, used by Harriet Tubman, among others, to signify to the fugitives at or near a station on the underground railroad that it was safe to come forth. Known for never losing a "passenger," it was she, Tubman, who was widely known among African Americans as "Moses." Then, too, we recall here, in conclusion, that in his biography of John Brown, Du Bois placed a pivotal quotation of Sojourner Truth's question to Frederick Douglass, in assembly at Salem, Massachusetts: "'Frederick, is God dead?'" As Du Bois gives it to us "'No,' thundered Douglass, towering above his Salem audience. 'No, and because God is not dead, slavery can only end in blood'" (Du Bois 1909, 122).

We may be given to understand that, *nonetheless*, they each—Sojourner Truth, Harriet Tubman, Frederick Douglass, John Brown, even W. E. B. Du Bois—went about *the work* of freedom.

We may say, in the context of Du Bois's references in his book *Color and Democracy*, completed at the outset of that fateful year of 1945, that they sought to join the natural and the supernatural, in their here, and their now.

We may say, finally, that they carried their work by way of a sense of hope, even an "unhopeful hope," as Du Bois had put it in *The Souls of Black Folk*. In such practice, belief in work well done expressed the lived sense that one could still rearticulate the meaning of "the starry skies," to quote at once the poet-composer from Bonn, the famous philosopher of Königsberg, and the African American writer-prophet interred at Accra—this time from here below, within the earth, even from beneath the ocean bottom, as exemplified in both the living and the dying of the massed millions, of Black folk, over the centuries. As they did in their way, so might we also seek a measure of peace. Let us name it here and now, as well as then and there, as futures, an *African* peace, *of* the limit of world. "Go Down Moses!"

Notes

Note to Incipit

1. Fred Moten, as always, helps us here; if my reading is apposite, we can place in parallax relation with what has been said so far his formulation of what is at stake: "the differentially repeating plane that intersects and animates the comparativist sphere" (Moten 2008, 1746).

Notes to Example

1. I reference here the work of two scholars, for example, as a liberal disposition in the criticism of Du Bois's thought on a world-historical horizon (Lewis 2000; Gallicchio 2000); and likewise, I note two exemplary scholars of a left-disposition (Horne 2004; Mullen 2005).

2. For all appearances, oriented toward Slavoj Žižek's appropriation of Karantani's suggestive intervention, Michael Hardt and Antonio Negri propose a critique of what they term a certain "parallelism" of political problematics—of the classic sort, as in class, race, gender, labor, and so on—in revolutionary struggle (Žižek 2006, cf. 17 and 362; Hardt & Negri 2009, 325–44). Yet, the misapprehension of the global order of problematic is mistaken perhaps within both of these discourses: a parallax is something quite other than a parallel—and not only in theory. Likewise, a sense of a "counter" modernity as it was proposed a half-generation ago in the discourse of Paul Gilroy, may yet still not recognize the historically constitutive character, according to Du Bois, precisely of the irruption of the problem of the color line as both limit and possibility, in the rendering of modernity as such (Gilroy 1993a). And still, proximate to a path that I would profoundly affirm of a thought beyond the traditional concept of contradiction within a dialectics marked by a heritage through Karl Marx from the thought of G. W. F. Hegel in the extraordinary projection of Fredric Jameson, it remains that what Du Bois has proposed as a thought of the double should be understood otherwise than a sense

of "duality" (for there is no stability of any term, or even the movement of the double in general, for it is certainly *never only double* even in the instance) (Jameson 2009, 219–20). As such, indeed, Du Bois's projection and indefatigable political practice across almost a century of decades, announced a disposition that Jameson would likely affirm, and should in all propriety be understood as a general form of critical intervention: a proposition of the possibility of the new as nonsimple, and hence never final, as such.

3. These remarks on the "problem of the color line" in Du Bois's thought draw essentially from my parallel remarks in a previously published essay on the place of Du Bois in the history of thought (Chandler 2006a, 40–45). This line of my own research on Du Bois was given renewed stimulation in the spring of 1999 by way of the kind invitation (personal correspondence) of the late Theodore Cross, then publisher of *Black Issues in Higher Education*, to consider commenting on Du Bois's most famous phrase "the problem of the twentieth century is the problem of the color line," on the occasion of the turn to the twenty-first century. It served as a provocation for a still ongoing reflection. While, I had certainly formulated the question of the twentieth century as but a "phase" of a larger and global problematic as early as 1991 (Chandler 1996, 265–66, note 2; Chandler 2014a, 70–74), it seemed to me that a sound-bite restatement of this thought was not so useful or appropriate. And such was all that I thought that I could manage at the time. I was chagrined to realize that the deep scholastic work on this fundamental motif had not yet been properly attempted by anyone, including me. Only now, a few years on, in the wake of my efforts at a certain necessary scholastic labor, do I feel that I can begin to contribute to an answer to Mr. Cross's solicitation (Du Bois 2015d; Chandler 2021).

4. And of course others have proposed the thought, based on Du Bois's own autobiographical statements, that such a global perspective was born from his experience in Europe as a student from 1892 to 1894. However, even this formulation is too simple. For Du Bois's apprehension of his experience in Europe was grounded in his ongoing and complicated critical engagement with the situation of the African American in the United States. I shall briefly explore one aspect of this question in the later stages of the present essay. The Pan-African Conference of 1900 was organized by the Trinidadian-born London-based barrister Henry Sylvester Williams as a founding member and leader of "The African Association," the latter of which should perhaps be considered a counter part to the American Negro Academy in the United States, for they were both founded in the same year and with a comparable project. Indeed, Sylvester Williams was in correspondence with African American leaders in the United States in formulating his association (Moss 1981, 54). See also Clarence Contee's early work on the history of the 1900 Pan-African Conference in London (Contee 1969a; Contee 1969b; Contee 1973).

5. Some of the writing of Paul Gilroy provides generalizable examples of both points. See in particular his discussion of the famous line as it appears in the

second chapter of *The Souls of Black Folk*, the chapter on the Freedmen's Bureau, in his widely read text from the early 1990s (Gilroy 1993b, 127).

6. In both senses Du Bois was the trailblazer. However, in our time, it is especially apposite to remark the latter. His work, in its persistence and scope, along with a deep philosophical grasp of the metaphysical dimensions of the problem of historicity that is often unremarked in the later literature, remains a high benchmark. The key texts include his major historical studies, from the doctoral dissertation from 1895 to his global account of the Negro from 1915, to his massive study of the meaning of Reconstruction in the United States from 1935 to his prescient and profound critique of the gathering horizon according to which a post–World War II global order was being instituted in 1945, as well as his biographical and fictional narratives, for example, *John Brown* (1909), *Dark Princess* (1928), and *The Black Flame: A Trilogy* (1957–61) (Du Bois 1973b; Du Bois 1975d; Du Bois 1976a; Du Bois 1973a; Du Bois 1974a; Du Bois 1976c; Du Bois 1976b; Du Bois 1976e). In this sense Du Bois's work can still be understood not only as a resource, whether affirmed or neglected, but as an interrogation in an epistemological sense of the work of recent scholars who have also proposed the decisive status of the processes of Atlantic slavery in a global history of modernity (Robinson [1983] 2000a; Rodney 1982; Blackburn 1988; Blackburn 1997a; Hall 1980; Holt 1992). Such point holds a fortiori for those scholars who address this question of slavery at the level of historicity itself in a somewhat indirect manner (Hardt & Negri 2000). And his definitive work preceded, and in part informed, the two classic interventions from the 1930s and 1940s concerning the role of slavery in the making of both the horizon for democratic revolutions of the nineteenth and twentieth centuries and in the making of capitalism generally as an historical form, C. L. R. James *The Black Jacobins* (1937) and Eric Williams *Capitalism and Slavery* (1944) (James 1989; Williams 1994); this is so despite or beyond the disputation of the fact of the well-known open-secret of James's claim that the Williams thesis was derived from his own tutelage of the latter (James 1972). While interventions are ongoing, one can note several respective summations of the debates in this domain among scholars of the immediate post-1960s intellectual generation (Darity 1988; Holt 1990; Blackburn 1997b; Klein 1999).

7. It perhaps should be underscored that the idea of *example* here is of anything but a pure idea. It should go without saying then that *exemplarity* can issue from multiple sites and situations, each with their revelatory and limiting capacities for thought, none of which are absolutely given. It is the responsibility of critical discourse to accept the task of thinking such a dynamic concept of limit.

8. And this affirmative concern with Africa on the part of Du Bois did not derive *simply* from the effect of his hearing Franz Boas praise ancient Africa during the anthropologist's 1906 commencement address at Atlanta University (a lecture that was given at the request of Du Bois). It can be shown that Du Bois had already proposed the central question, the possibility of an affirmation of the

history of ancient Africa, as well as this thetic response in statements across his work from 1897 to 1905 (Contee 1969a; Contee 1969b; Contee 1973).

9. And, then, one can find an even more complicated contrapuntal form of renarrativization across *The Black Flame Trilogy* of the last years of Du Bois's life (Du Bois 1976c; Du Bois 1976b; Du Bois 1976f). This late gesture requires its own sustained treatment, and I propose to offer such elsewhere.

10. Scholarship in this domain has usually rather resolutely taken as its problematic the question "what is the influence of Europe on Du Bois?" The way in which Du Bois proposed a thinking of the historicity of Europe has usually remained just outside of the principle of interpretation for this literature, especially on his relation to Germany. A partial exception can be recognized in a relatively recent essay by Michael Rothberg on the holocaust and memory (2001); perhaps it is a sign of changes that are afoot.

11. Alternately titled "Africa *and* the French Revolution" or "The Negro *in* the French Revolution" (my emphasis in both cases), this text was first published in the summer 1961 issue of the journal *Freedomways*, under the title "Africa and the French Revolution," just months before Du Bois emigrated to Ghana, West Africa (Du Bois 1961). It was republished the following year as a pamphlet in Lagos, Nigeria (with the first title mentioned above on the title page and the second one on an inside cover page). This latter publication can now be found in the microfilm edition of the W. E. B. Du Bois Papers (Du Bois 1980a). The 1961 publication was reprinted in the 1970 celebrative collection *Black Titan* by the editors of Freedomways, the latter of which was drawn in the main from a 1965 special issue in the same journal (Du Bois 1970). Although Herbert Aptheker's annotated bibliography lists the item, citing the Lagos publication, the text, from either source, is apparently not included in any of the volumes of Du Bois's Complete Published Works that was edited by him.

12. In this light, it can be said that the more recent engagements of this question, for example those put forth by Bill V. Mullen and Marc S. Gallicchio, along with the biographical account given by David Levering Lewis, are marked by this double confusion, or the persisting obscurity of their own formulations in this domain (Mullen 2004; Gallicchio 2000; Lewis 2002; Lewis 2000). And, other relevant scholarship in the American context can be indexed by way of their interventions. What is obscure in their presentation of Du Bois's discourse is precisely the fundamental sense—the deep historical sense of *problem*—and its epistemic implication, as it is produced within his own enunciation. Thus, while Mullen has edited a collection of some of the writings of Du Bois pertaining to this matter, he frames his presentation in such a preemptive manner that those aspects of the older thinker's discourse which cannot be grasped in the most immediately direct and summary fashion remain in essence illegible for critical engagement (Du Bois 2005). Ultimately, the presentation given in Mullen's account is unable to resolve a central conundrum with regard to Du Bois that is generated by his approach. If

a contemporary scholar, such as Mullen, wishes to withdraw from Japan's history during the first half of the twentieth century (and we should, and I do along with him) and would yet seek to affirm a vision of China after the Second World War as the proper hope of the future (as he implies), how does one address at the level of Du Bois's own thought his persistent *simultaneous* affirmation of Japan and China after the Second World War, that is, as an octogenarian, in which such affirmation was constitutively related to its simultaneity? (And this is not to gainsay the open question of our own contemporary critical understanding of China.) Yet, too, with regard to both Lewis and Gallicchio, respectively, the presumptive truth of a supposed liberal internationalism (in relation to a kind of supposed or ostensible parochial internationalism), can be understood in turn to subtend the passively stated but still categorical strictures against Du Bois's discourse on Asia, especially his statements on Japan. Thus, what these two writers seem unable to reckon with is the constitutive epistemic limit that they inhabit along with Du Bois: that there is no outside standpoint from which to adjudge this scene (a planetary or global one); and, hence in their declared statements on Du Bois, they seem unable to consider (or remain unaware of) the possibility that liberalism in all of its inter-related blindness and insight may not be able to account for the conditions of its own emergence and vocative stance. That is, it does not arise apart from but rather is *of*—both from and about—the modern history of systems of hierarchy, notably imperialism, as the production of the modern "problem of the color line" as Du Bois elaborated it across some six decades. Hence such liberalism is indeed an interested and partial position; and this partiality remains despite any claim of an orientation toward a universal horizon of value. There is no neutral, safe, or pure, position from which one can adjudge the unfolding of historicity. Like Du Bois, the discourse of these two writers is an attempt to intervene in the horizon of the problematic (including discourse) set afoot by way of modern imperial and colonial practice. In contradistinction to these two authors then, Du Bois's practice brings into relief the question of the relation of the epistemic position of a discourse that presumes a whole or a limit (such as a so-called global perspective or a supposed planetary one), on the one hand, and the whole question that goes under the name of sovereignty in contemporary thought, on the other. This is a domain of paradox and the unavoidable contradiction of thought and practice. Accordingly, the openness of Du Bois's discourse to this profound difficulty—which arises for all practice in this dimension of existence—his simultaneous withdrawal from the fiction of neutrality that is presumptive in a certain liberalism (in the judgments against him proposed by Gallicchio and Lewis, for example) and his commitment to a futural horizon of sovereign responsibility beyond what has yet been in the past or present will likely prove more supple for our thinking of the future(s) of Asia, including Japan and China, as well as India, Indonesia, Vietnam, and so forth, not to gainsay the world in general. What can hardly be remarked by these latter two authors is the extent to which the world in which we now exist, which is unavoidably the scene of our departure into any future, has been made by a certain and quite specific history: as such, it can offer no ultimate ground for judgment. We (they along with me) inhabit this difficulty along with Du Bois (Chandler 2012a).

Notes to Exemplarity

1. Elsewhere, I have elaborated this necessity of such real fictions in practical-theoretical labor as given in the problematic of Du Bois (Chandler 2008; Chandler 2014a). Whereas, I believe such theoretical work must, of necessity, occur without or beyond any name, as such, it remains that if we take it as other than a thought of the historial as oriented first of all or ultimately by existence as being, I would propose to think of the concern of such practice as *paraontological*. As an additional annotation, I can note that the thought and term *theoretical fiction* takes resource from Gayatri Spivak's formulation and engagement of this problematic a generation past, specifically in her reading of the subaltern studies question in colonial India (Spivak 1988). In turn, there, she references Sigmund Freud's formulation—in the closing section of his watershed discourse on the "interpretation of dreams"—of the aconceptual concept of the "unconscious" by way of his thinking through of the limits of consciousness, in which therefrom, the thought of the unconscious is such a theoretical fiction (Freud [1900] 1965). Here, I am concerned to accent such supposed theoretical disposition and premise as always and first, so to speak, practical, the practical theoretical. In my ongoing meditations on this problematic, referenced in this note above, in part, such question definitively marks the whole terrain of a politics that might address our common colonial and postcolonial nexus on a worldwide ensemble of horizons.

2. This phrase is a turn on a formulation by Du Bois—"rivers of Gold"—from "The Development of a People," an essay that followed in 1904 hard on the heels of his assemblage of *The Souls of Black Folk* in early 1903. On the event of the purchase of that original group of Africans, a bit of gold dust entered the exchange and sparked the imagination of the trading Portuguese. A watercourse nearby to the event off the coast of northwest Africa entered the European discourses as Rio do Ouro, or the river of gold. General historiography remarks well the depth at which the gold dust received by that key trader, Antonio Gonçalves, sparked renewed exploratory expeditions throughout much of Europe (Vincent 1807, 217). Here, Du Bois annotates that it was the ensuing trade in humans that comprised a "river of Gold." The essay in question, this phrase in particular, articulates in its own cadence the resonant depths of Du Bois's conception of slavery as constitutive of the modern global historical horizon. It is one in which the first date given above, 1442, maybe understood as a theoretical metaphor of this situation: in which modern slavery stands at the inception—neither inside nor outside—of modern imperial colonialism, of a supposed European world economy, of capitalism as a system, of modernity as a global horizon (Du Bois 1904, 299, para. 17; Du Bois

2015b; Lach 1965, 50–58; Galvão 1731, 23; Galvão 1601, 27).

3. Here, too, it may be of general epistemological interest to index in all its complexity the way in which Du Bois adduces the theoretical implication of this thought in his reading of Japan's imperial aggressions in China across the first half of the twentieth century. As noted above, during and following his visits to both China and Japan in late 1936, Du Bois wrote a series of texts describing his sense of each country and his understanding of both of their places, respectively, in modern history and their relation to each other. Across the first half of 1937, following his visit to East Asia, the Second Sino-Japanese War erupted. In the September 1937 issue of the *Pittsburgh Courier* (perhaps the premier newspaper of the first half of the twentieth century edited by and oriented toward African Americans), a paper in which Du Bois maintained a weekly column at the time, after having written eight columns on these counties during the first half of the year, following the eruption of war, he was led to propose a historical perspective on its genesis. While a further critical account and reflection on Du Bois's approach to this historical topography in general must be developed elsewhere, his direct statements on the outbreak of the Second Sino-Japanese War and Japan's aggressions in China, which were at once imperial and colonial, engineered by military force, were fortunately registered in the pages of the *Pittsburgh Courier* columns in September and October of 1937 and should be annotated here. For, as presented by Du Bois, they articulate in stark, dense, and profound sense, the deep torsions of historicity that he understood to be at stake in the devolutions of power and economy across Northeast Asia during that time. Du Bois claimed as the opening orientation of the September 25th column that in the conflict "we see the forerunners of that great change in the world's center which is going eventually—not, of course, this decade or this century—but eventually, to make Asia the center of the world again, which is its natural place" (Du Bois 1937, para. 1). He then recalls an argument that he had proposed in the earlier columns (and which he developed in writings on Japan that he completed in 1937, but which remained unpublished at the time and are only now coming into print) that the rise of Japan since the 1890s had frustrated the imperial ambitions of Europe in Asia. Indexing the imperial ambition of Japan, he notes that since that decade (if not beforehand), Japan "has been determined to achieve her economic independence of the Western world by dominating the policies and resources of China" (Du Bois 1937, para. 2). Thus, as the First World War led Europe to a pause in its efforts to subsume China within its projection, Japan seized the moment. And further, he wrote, a whole set of historical possibility might have opened if "Russia and China could have made common ground for the emancipation of the working classes of the world," for then "two thirds of the world would have been arrayed against the industrial imperialism of Europe." However, in Du Bois's view the loss of "the great and farsighted leader Sun Yatsen" opened the way in China for a leadership that turned "in reality toward the leadership of modern industrial imperialism as [it was then] represented in China, especially by England" (Du Bois 1937, para. 4). In the same historical unfolding, the West, that

is, Europe and America, began a hidden economic "attack" on Japan by raising the price of the raw materials that it needed for industrialization, cotton, iron, and so on, which, in Du Bois's view in this column, led Japan to seek other secure sources for such materials, that is, in its eventuality "the annexation of North China" (Du Bois 1937, para. 5). Thus, comes Du Bois's interpretation of Japan's motive in instituting that war. "It is to escape annihilation and subjection and the nameless slavery of Western Europe that Japan has gone into a horrible and bloody carnage with her own cousin; but the cause and the blame for this war lies in England, and France, and America; on Germany and Italy; on all those white nations, which for a hundred years and more have by blood and rapine forced their rule upon colored nations" (Du Bois 1937, para. 6). Thus, Du Bois proposed that Japan's aggression in China should be understood as "self-defense" against the threat of domination by Europe's imperial states. In this sense, he adjudged that the war that erupted on Chinese soil in July 1937 was "one of the great deciding wars of the world and the future of colored people is bound up with it" (Du Bois 1937, para. 6). Finally, bringing to full point the theorization that guided his reading of modern historicity in this consideration, recalling his visit to Shanghai in November of 1936, he wrote in the first person that "I stood a year ago [where bombs have since fallen] . . . in the midst of the International Settlement," the domain of the infamous foreign extraterritorial concessions that were inaugurated in the nineteenth century, and that "I knew then, as I know now, that the present war in Asia has as its decisive cause the African slave trade and the Industrial Revolution of Europe" (Du Bois 1937, para. 7). These remarks are excerpted from my introduction to the publication of three texts by Du Bois on Japan and China, written in 1936 and 1937, previously unpublished, which are forthcoming (Du Bois 2012c; Du Bois 2012a; Du Bois 2012b; Chandler 2012a; Chandler 2012b).

4. In "The African Diaspora," a brief companion text to the present essay, which I prepared for and presented at the inaugural symposium of the project "Issues in Critical Investigation: The African Diaspora," held September 30–October 2, 2011, convened at Vanderbilt University by Hortense Spillers under the nominal auspices of the Department of English there; the idea of possibility adduced here is remarked a bit further (Chandler 2014b).

5. In his work of the 1970s and early 1980s, Cedric Robinson annotated that Du Bois's published formulation of the term an "aristocracy of labor" predated by more than a year, at least, the usage of the same formulation (but with different theoretical valence) by Vladimir Lenin (Robinson [1983] 2000a, 328n69). And I should note that one can already find this thought fully afoot in Du Bois discourse from the midpoint of the first decade of the new century (Du Bois 1906b; Du Bois 2006; Du Bois 1909, chaps. 12 and 13).

6. Perhaps here it matters to notate that this horizon as we are outlining it both affirms and solicits the kind of formulation of question adduced in the work of Étienne Balibar across the past two decades (Balibar 2004). In addition, one might

consider the recent propositions of Sandro Mezzadra on the necessity of elaborating a retheorization of the place of so-called primary or primitive accumulation within the contemporary historicity of capitalism to provide a distinct and fundamental intervention on this same terrain (Mezzadra 2011; Mezzadra 2010). And, it is here too that I note the signal theoretical-interpretive amplification of the contemporary horizon in the ongoing work of Nicholas De Genova, here taking note especially of his reference to the 2006 mobilizations against new immigration policies in the United States (De Genova 2010). We find therein his recollection of the marvelously imperturbable, and thus empowering, phrases of new possibilities for our time "*¡Aquí Estamos, y No Nos Vamos!*" (Here we are, and we're not leaving!) and "*¡Y Si Nos Sacan, Nos Regresamos!*" [And if they throw us out, we'll come right back!]. For this phrase may be understood to suggest that at the moment that the imperial figure (Portugal, Spain, England, Italy, France, Germany, Japan, the United States, etc.) announced itself as "the stranger knocking at the gate" of its supposed new subjects, the country that such putative supraordinate figure called home ceased to belong only to him. Yet, with an historical ear, we likewise annotate in this context such future already being projected in the question with which Du Bois closed *The Souls of Black Folk: Essays and Sketches* in 1903—"Your country? How came it yours?"—as a world-historical question, one that had indeed already been posed in the context of "America" at the opening of the century before his enunciation, if not earlier (Du Bois 1903d, 262, chap. 14, para. 25). It now can be understood to bear its historical resonance from one opening of a new century (at 1900, in both temporal directions) to the next (at 2000, in both temporal directions), from one idiom of discourse and language to another (in both linguistic directions): "*¡Aquí Estamos, y No Nos Vamos! ¡Y Si Nos Sacan, Nos Regresamos!*"

7. This paragraph, along with the following sentences in this note, in fact opened my presentation of parts of this text at Queen Mary University of London in October 2011. At its most fundamental level, this exorbitance of our question is what I propose as the implication of Denise Ferreira da Silva's pathbreaking study *Toward a Global Idea of Race*, noted above (Silva 2007). In related but diverse senses, it is what I take to be the considered implication of the most recent and ongoing itineraries of three intellectuals from three different generations of radical thought, also now working in Europe—Nicholas De Genova, Sandro Mezzadra, and Étienne Balibar (each cited above or below in this text). This, it must be fully understood, is a formulation and placement of the work of these scholars according to my own disposition; and no presumption should be made that they will recognize my reference as their own as such. And yet—in continuity of implication with the references just given—the revolution, in theory, has begun. Thus, as well, I mention here, within the horizon of a problematic that I will specifically register as the *question* of the "African Diaspora," an ensemble of names that are essential for my formation or of my generation—within the horizon of the United States:

not only, Cedric Robinson (noted above), but also Hortense Spillers (2003a) and Lucius Outlaw (1996); and then, Fred Moten (2003), Ronald A. T. Judy (1993), Saidiya Hartman (1997), Lewis Ricardo Gordon (2008), and Frank Wilderson III (2010). These references name, for me, a contemporary horizon as task, as a demand for a certain labor of thought: that is, a paleonymic practice in the interstices of the living future of the historical present. It is in this sense that I outline in the context of our discussion—as a certain form of rememorization—the principle of a critical history of the "colors" of "labor power" by way of reference to W. E. B. Du Bois's formulation of a thought of the global "problem of the color line," from the turn of the century certainly, but especially across the time of the two World Wars, with implications right up to our most contemporary moment.

8. Hence, paradoxically, it has a continued solicitation of the discourses concerning Africa. It stands just outside of the project of "an invention of Africa." It is already an example of the critique of discourses that is later proposed by Michel Foucault (1973) and Valentin Mudimbe (1988). Historiography in the general philosophical and political sense that I have outlined here is the principal concern of this text.

9. I reserve for another context a patient tracking of the interwoven character and implication of these two references, to two Greek myths, to the mythic order in the context of historiography, to both an "Africa" and an "African America," to "the Negro" and to "Black Folk," to Greece and Africa, including its Diaspora (see Annotation II).

10. In his introduction to the 1976 reissue of *The World and Africa*, Herbert Aptheker quotes from the initial letter that Du Bois addressed to Viking Press on January 17, 1945 proposing the idea for this book "title to be 'The Africas' emphasizing the fact that Africa is not one country, one group or one race but a conglomerate of peoples with various degrees of importance and possibilities who are going to play roles in the post-war world" (Du Bois 1976d, 5; Du Bois 1997, 29). It may be that China will come to be understood as "not one country, one group or one race but a conglomerate of peoples," afoot in the planetary horizon of the twenty-first century and beyond. This question, this difficult possibility, may be constitutive of the present form of this problem of the centuries. Contemporary scholarship has begun to offer us a salutary perspective with regard to historical China in the twenty-first century and beyond—the profound sense of the multiplicities within its proclaimed purview (Gladney 2004; Rossabi 2004; Evans, Hutton, & Kuah 2000; see also Annotation II).

Note to Repassage

1. The quotation is given by Du Bois as being from "Swinburne 'The Garden of Proserpine'" (Swinburne 1904).

Note on Citations

While I have taken scholastic references from the original publications, or the unpublished manuscripts, of texts by W. E. B. Du Bois, in every case, with citations thereto as noted within the texts, where possible or appropriate, I have without exception also consulted, and often cited, primarily the version of any text included in the thirty-seven volumes of The Complete Published Works of W. E. B. Du Bois, published by the Kraus-Thomson Organization, edited and introduced by the late Herbert Aptheker, from 1973 to 1986; the six volumes of Du Bois's texts published by the University of Massachusetts Press, also edited and introduced by Aptheker; three of selected correspondence; and three of selections of other texts, including previously unpublished texts and documents, from 1973 to 1985. Specific bibliographical details for the texts cited from among these volumes can be found in the list of references at the end of this study.

The Souls of Black Folk: Essays and Sketches, is cited herein from the first edition of its original publication (Du Bois 1903d); the second edition, which has no major changes from the first, is available as an open-access text online in a scholastically reliable electronic form (Du Bois 1903c). The pagination is the same for both editions.

With *Dusk of Dawn: Autobiography of a Race Concept*, originally published in 1940 (Du Bois 1940), when quoting or referencing specific passages of the text, I have cited herein from its 1975 reprint as a volume in the Complete Published Works series indicated above (Du Bois 1975c). While the 1975 edition is not a facsimile of the 1940 first edition, its pagination follows exactly that of the first edition. Since pagination varies somewhat among the multiple and most commonly accessible editions of this text, I underscore here as an aid to the reader, that within my text I usually indicate the title of the chapter, or note the subsection thereof, that is under discussion. In the text below, I privilege and cite here the 1975

Kraus-Thomson edition as edited by Aptheker—by Du Bois's family name, year of publication of that edition, followed by page number(s) (e.g., Du Bois 1975c, 26–27, 13–15, 51–52, 54).

In addition, for several early essays by Du Bois, while I always cite them according to their original publication or manuscript (details for which may be found in the reference list for the book as a whole) with regard to quotation or reference to specific passages within the essays, I also always cite the paragraph number within the relevant essay. Since these essays are most often also included in *The Problem of the Color Line at the Turn of the Twentieth Century: The Essential Early Essays* (Fordham University Press, 2015), wherein the paragraph enumeration is included in the margins for each essay, any reader may easily take exact reference to this edition of the texts by way of these citations of the paragraph in question (Du Bois 2015e). Notably, "The Present Outlook for the Dark Races of Mankind" is first cited by its original publication, followed by the paragraph number (e.g., Du Bois 1900, 95, para. 1), with an additional citation to the newly reedited and annotated version of this essay in *The Problem of the Color Line at the Turn of the Twentieth Century: The Essential Early Essays*. The essays included in that book collection are each complete (as originally published or as extant in the unpublished papers of W. E. B. Du Bois), edited and annotated, according to contemporary scholarship. As appropriate, after the abbreviation and the page number, I cite the relevant paragraph number within that original version of the essay (enumeration begins from the first paragraph indentation mark from a count of number one).

I occasionally make reference to material that may be found only (as original documents or in microfilm form derived therefrom) among the Papers of W. E. B. Du Bois, Special Collections and University Archives, Series 3, Subseries C, MS 312, University of Massachusetts Libraries, housed in the W. E. B. Du Bois Library at the University of Massachusetts, Amherst. Currently maintained by the Department of Special Collections and University Archives of the University of Massachusetts Libraries, the original papers were compiled and edited by Herbert Aptheker, whereas the microfilm edition was supervised by Robert C. McDonnell. Relevant bibliographic detail for the latter kind of citations may be found in the reference list at the end of the study, which also includes a notation for the microfilm edition of these papers (Du Bois 1980b). All of those papers, in essence, are now available as open-access material (in principle, available for access from anywhere at any time), via the University of Massachusetts Libraries, W. E. B. Du Bois Library, Special Collections and Archives (SCUA), online portal, which was inaugurated under the name of CREDO.

References

Adelson, Leslie. 2005. "Toward a New Critical Grammar of Migration." In *The Turkish Turn in Contemporary German Literature: Toward a New Critical Grammar of Migration*, 1–30. New York: Palgrave Macmillan.

Althusser, Louis. 1997. "From Capital to Marx's Philosophy." In *Reading Capital*, by L. Althusser and Étienne Balibar, 13–69. Translated by Ben Brewster. London New York: Verso.

Anderson, Marian. 1939. "Marian Anderson Performs on the Steps of the Lincoln Memorial: With an Introduction by Harold Ickes." Records of the Office of the Secretary of the Interior, United States National Archives. Audiotape/ reel recording. https://catalog.archives.gov/OpaAPI/media/1729137/content/ arcmedia/mopix/audio/ww2/48-223.mp3.

———. (1936) 1999. "Go Down Moses." In *Spirituals*. Franz Rupp, pianist. Sony Classical Records.

Aptheker, Herbert. 1975. Introduction. In *Color and Democracy: Colonies and Peace*, edited by Herbert Aptheker, by W. E. B. Du Bois, 5–18. Millwood, NY: Kraus-Thomson.

———. 1976. Introduction. In *The World and Africa: An Inquiry into the Part which Africa Has Played in World History*, edited by H. Aptheker, by W. E. B. Du Bois, 5–20. Millwood, NY: Kraus-Thomas.

Arrighi, Giovanni. 2002. "Lineages of Empire." *Philosophia Africana* 5, no. 2 (August): 13–23.

———. 2007. *Adam Smith in Beijing: Lineages of the Twenty-first Century*. London, New York: Verso.

Balibar, Étienne. 2004. *We, the People of Europe? Reflections on Transnational Citizenship*. Princeton, NJ: Princeton University Press.

Barenboim, Daniel. 2012. *Barenboim on Beethoven: Nine Symphonies that Changed the World*. Film. Directed by Michael Waldman. West-Eastern Divan Orchestra. London: Rare Day-Independent Production.

Beethoven, Ludwig van. 2014. Symphony No. 9 in D Minor, op. 125. Chicago Symphony Orchestra and Chorus, Riccardo Muti. Performed September 18.

Chicago: Chicago Symphony Organization. Video, 121 min., 22 sec. https://cso.org/watch/; https://youtu.be/rOjHhS5MtvA.

Bible. 1966. *The Jerusalem Bible*. Edited and translated by Alexander Jones, et al. Garden City, NY: Doubleday.

Blackburn, Robin. 1988. *The Overthrow of Colonial Slavery, 1776–1848*. London, New York: Verso.

———. 1997a. *The Making of New World Slavery: From the Baroque to the Modern, 1492–1800*. London, New York: Verso.

———. 1997b. "New World Slavery, Primitive Accumulation and British Industrialization." In *The Making of New World Slavery: From the Baroque to the Modern, 1492–1800*, 509–80. London, New York: Verso.

Butler, Judith. 2004. *Undoing Gender*. Boca Raton, FL: Routledge, Taylor & Francis.

———. 2009. *Frames of War: When Is Life Grievable?* London, New York: Verso.

Chandler, Nahum Dimitri. 1993. "Between." *Assemblage: A Critical Journal of Architecture and Design Culture* 20 (April): 26–27.

———. 1996. "The Figure of the X: An Elaboration of the Du Boisian Autobiographical Example." In *Displacement, Diaspora, and Geographies of Identity*, edited by Smadar Lavie and Ted Swedenburg, 235–72. Durham, NC: Duke University Press.

———. 2006a. "The Figure of W. E. B. Du Bois as a Problem for Thought." "W. E. B. Du Bois and the Question of Another World," edited by N. D. Chandler. Special issue, *CR: New Centennial Review* 6, no. 3 (Winter): 29–55.

———. 2006b. "The Possible Form of an Interlocution: W. E. B. Du Bois and Max Weber in Correspondence, 1904–1905, Part I: The Letters and the Essay." "W. E. B. Du Bois and the Question of Another World," edited by N. D. Chandler. Special issue, *CR: New Centennial Review* 6, no. 3 (Winter): 193–239.

———. 2007. "The Possible Form of an Interlocution: W. E. B. Du Bois and Max Weber in Correspondence, 1904–1905, Part II: The Terms of Discussion." *CR: New Centennial Review* 7, no. 1 (Spring): 213–72.

———. 2008. "Of Exorbitance: The Problem of the Negro as a Problem for Thought." *Criticism: A Quarterly Journal for Literature and the Arts* 50, no. 3: 345–410.

———. 2012a. "Introduction: On the Virtues of Seeing—At Least, but Never only—Double." "Toward a New Parallax: Or, Japan—In Another Traversal of the Trans-Pacific." Special issue, *CR: New Centennial Review* 12, no. 1 (Spring): 1–39.

———. 2012b. "A Persistent Parallax: On W. E. B. Du Bois's Writings on Japan and China, 1936–1937." "Toward a New Parallax: Or, Japan—In Another Traversal of the Trans-Pacific." Special issue, *CR: New Centennial Review* 12, no. 1 (Spring): 291–316.

———. 2014a. "Of Exorbitance: The Problem of the Negro as a Problem for Thought." In *X: The Problem of the Negro as a Problem for Thought*, 11–67. New York: Fordham University Press.

———. 2014b. "Parenthesis." In *X: The Problem of the Negro as a Problem for Thought*, 171–77. New York: Fordham University Press.

———. 2018. "The Coming of the Second Time." *A-Line: A Journal of Progressive Thought* 1, nos. 3–4. https://alinejournal.com/.

———. 2021. *"Beyond this Narrow Now": Or, Delimitations, of W. E. B. Du Bois*. Durham, NC: Duke University Press.

———. Forthcoming. *Annotations on the Early Thought of W. E. B. Du Bois and the Discourses of the Negro*. Durham, NC: Duke University Press.

Contee, Clarence G. 1969a. "The Emergence of W. E. B. Du Bois as an African Nationalist." *Journal of Negro History* 54, no. 1 (January): 48–63.

———. 1969b. *W. E. B Du Bois and African Nationalism, 1914–1945*. PhD diss. Washington, DC: American University.

———. 1973. *Henry Sylvester Williams and Origins of Organizational Pan-Africanism, 1897–1902*. Washington, DC: Howard University.

Dante. (ca. 1320) 1999. *Divina Commedia*. Edited by Giorgio Petrocchi. Translated by Robert Hollander and Jean Hollander. Princeton University. https://dante.princeton.edu/index.html.

Darity, William. 1988. "The Williams Thesis before Williams." *Slavery and Abolition* 9: 29–41.

Davis, Angela Y. 1998. *Blues Legacies and Black Feminism: Gertrude "Ma" Rainey, Bessie Smith, and Billie Holiday*. New York: Pantheon Books.

De Genova, Nicholas. 2010. "The Queer Politics of Migration: Reflections on 'Illegality' and Incorrigibility." *Studies in Social Justice* 4, no. 2: 101–26.

Derrida, Jacques. 1976. *Of Grammatology*. Translated by G. C. Spivak. Baltimore: Johns Hopkins University Press.

Du Bois, W. E. B. 1900. "The Present Outlook for the Dark Races of Mankind." *A. M. E. Church Review* 17, no. 2 (66): 95–110.

———. 1901. "The Freedmen's Bureau." *The Atlantic Monthly: A Magazine of Literature, Science, Art, and Politics* 87, no. 519 (March): 354–65.

———. 1903a. "Of the Meaning of Progress." In *The Souls of Black Folk: Essays and Sketches*. 1st ed., 60–74. Chicago: A. C. McClurg.

———. 1903b. "Of the Passing of the First Born." In *The Souls of Black Folk: Essays and Sketches*. 1st ed., 207–14. Chicago: A. C. McClurg.

———. 1903c. *The Souls of Black Folk: Essays and Sketches*. 2nd ed. Documenting the American South: University Library, University of North Carolina at Chapel Hill, 2001. http://docsouth.unc.edu/church/duboissouls/dubois.html.

———. 1903d. *The Souls of Black Folk: Essays and Sketches*. 1st ed. Chicago: A. C. McClurg.

———. 1904. "The Development of a People." *International Journal of Ethics* 14 (April): 292–311.

———. 1906a. "The Color Line Belts the World." *Collier's Weekly* 28 (October 20): 20.

———. 1906b. "Die Negerfrage in den Vereinigten Staaten." *Archiv Für Sozialwissenschaft und Sozialpolitik* 22 (January): 31–79.

———. 1909. *John Brown*. Philadelphia: G. W. Jacobs.

———. 1910. "The Souls of White Folk." *Independent* 69 (August 18): 339–42.

———. 1915. "The African Roots of War." *Atlantic Monthly* 115, no. 5, May: 707–14.

———. 1917. "Of the Culture of White Folk." *Journal of Race Development* 7 (April): 434–47.

———. 1920a. *Darkwater: Voices from within the Veil*. New York: Harcourt, Brace and Howe.

———. Ca. 1920b. "Story: The Secret Singer." Special Collections and University Archives, University of Massachusetts Amherst. Papers.

———. 1928. *Dark Princess: A Romance*. New York: Harcourt, Brace.

———. 1935. *Black Reconstruction: An Essay toward a History of the Part which Black Folk Played in the Attempt to Reconstruct Democracy in America, 1860–1880*. New York: Harcourt, Brace.

———. 1937. Forum of Fact and Opinion. *Pittsburgh Courier*, September 25.

———. 1940. *Dusk of Dawn: An Essay toward an Autobiography of a Race Concept*. New York: Harcourt, Brace.

———. 1945. *Color and Democracy: Colonies and Peace*. New York: Harcourt, Brace.

———. 1947. *The World and Africa: An Inquiry into the Part which Africa Has Played in World History*. New York: Viking Press.

———. 1957–61. *The Black Flame: A Trilogy*. New York: Mainstream Publishers.

———. 1961. Africa and the French Revolution. *Freedomways: A Quarterly Review of the Negro Freedom Movement* 1, no. 2 (Summer): 136–51.

———. 1962. *Africa and the French Revolution*. Lagos, Nigeria: Megida Printers and Publishers.

———. 1968. *The Autobiography of W. E. B. Du Bois: A Soliloquy on Viewing My Life from the Last Decade of Its First Century*. Edited by H. Aptheker. New York: International Publishers.

———. 1970. "Africa and the French Revolution." In *Black Titan, W.E.B. Du Bois: An Anthology by the Editors of Freedomways*, J. H. Clarke, E. Jackson, E. Kaiser, and J. O'Dell, 241–57. Boston, MA: Beacon Press.

———. 1973a. *John Brown*. Edited by H. Aptheker. Millwood, NY: Kraus-Thomson.

———. 1973b. *The Suppression of the African Slave-Trade to the United States of America, 1638–1870*. Edited by H. Aptheker. Millwood, NY: Kraus-Thomson.

———. 1974a. *Dark Princess: A Romance*. Edited by H. Aptheker. NY: Kraus-Thomson.

———. 1974b. *The Quest of the Silver Fleece: A Novel*. Edited by H. Aptheker. Millwood, NY: Kraus-Thomson.

———. 1975a. *Color and Democracy: Colonies and Peace*. Edited by Herbert Aptheker. Millwood, NY: Kraus-Thomson.

———. 1975b. *Darkwater: Voices from within the Veil*. Edited by H. Aptheker. Millwood, NY: Kraus-Thomson.

———. 1975c. *Dusk of Dawn: An Essay toward an Autobiography of a Race Concept.* Edited by H. Aptheker. Millwood, NY: Kraus-Thomson.

———. 1975d. *The Negro.* Edited by H. Aptheker. Millwood, NY: Kraus-Thomson.

———. 1975e. "The Shadow of Years." In *Darkwater: Voices from within the Veil*, edited by H. Aptheker, 5–23. Millwood, NY: Kraus-Thomson.

———. 1976a. *Black Reconstruction: An Essay toward a History of the Part which Black Folk Played in the Attempt to Reconstruct Democracy in America, 1860–1880.* Edited by H. Aptheker. Millwood, NY: Kraus-Thomson.

———. 1976b. *The Black Flame: A Trilogy. Vol. 2, Mansart Builds a School.* Edited by H. Aptheker. W. E. B. Du Bois. Millwood, NY: Kraus-Thomson.

———. 1976c. *The Black Flame: A trilogy. Vol. 1, The Ordeal of Mansart.* Edited by H. Aptheker. Millwood, NY: Kraus-Thomson.

———. 1976d. *The World and Africa: An Inquiry into the Part which Africa Has Played in World History.* Edited by H. Aptheker. Millwood, NY: Kraus-Thomson.

———. 1976e. *The Black Flame: A Trilogy. Vol. 3, Worlds of Color.* Edited by H. Aptheker. Millwood, NY: Kraus-Thomson.

———. 1980a. "Africa and the French Revolution." In *The Papers of W. E. B. Du Bois, 1803 (1877–1963) 1965*, compiled and edited by H. Aptheker. Sanford, NC: Microfilming Corp. of America.

———. 1980b. *The Papers of W. E. B. Du Bois, 1803 (1877–1963) 1979.* Compiled and edited by H. Aptheker and Robert C. McDonnell. Sanford, NC: Microfilming Corp. of America.

———. 1980c. "Testimony Concerning the Charter of the United Nations." In *Contributions by W. E. B. Du Bois in Government Publications and Proceedings*, edited by H. Aptheker, 383–87. Millwood, NY: Kraus-Thomson.

———. 1980d. "A World Search for Democracy." Unpublished manuscript in *The Papers of W. E. B. Du Bois, 1803 (1877–1963) 1979.* Sanford, NC: Microfilming Corp. of America.

———. 1982a. "The African Roots of War." In *Writings by W. E. B. Du Bois in Periodicals Edited by Others. Vol. 2, 1910–1934*, compiled and edited by H. Aptheker, 96–104. Millwood, NY: Kraus-Thomson.

———. 1982b. "China and Africa." In *Writings by W. E. B. Du Bois in Periodicals Edited by Others. Vol. 4, 1945–1961*, compiled and edited by H. Aptheker, 292–95. Millwood, NY: Kraus-Thomson.

———. 1982c. "Imperialism, United Nations, Colonial People." In *Writings by W. E. B. Du Bois in Periodicals Edited by Others. Vol. 3, 1935–1944*, compiled and edited by H. Aptheker, 225–28. Millwood, NY: Kraus-Thomson.

———. 1982d. "The Pan-African Movement." In *Writings by W. E. B. Du Bois in Non-periodical Literature Edited by Others*, edited and compiled by H. Aptheker, 242–52. Millwood, NY: Kraus-Thomson.

———. 1982e. "A Program of Emancipation for Colonial Peoples. In *Writings by W. E. B. Du Bois in Non-periodical Literature Edited by Others*, edited and compiled by H. Aptheker, 259–64. Millwood, NY: Kraus-Thomson.

———. 1982f. "Worlds of Color." In *Writings by W. E. B. Du Bois in Periodicals Edited by Others. Vol. 2, 1910–1934*, compiled and edited by H. Aptheker, 241–56. Millwood, NY: Kraus-Thomson.

———. 1983. "Marxism and the Negro Question." In *Selections from the Crisis. Vol. 2, 1926–1934*, compiled and edited by H. Aptheker, 695–99. Millwood, NY: Kraus-Thomson.

———. 1985a. "The Art and Art Galleries of Modern Europe." In *Against Racism: Unpublished Essays, Papers, Addresses, 1887–1961*, edited by H. Aptheker, 33–43. Amherst: University of Massachusetts Press.

———. 1985b. "The Spirit of Modern Europe." In *Against Racism Unpublished Essays, Papers, Addresses, 1887–1961*, edited by H. Aptheker, 50–64. Amherst: University of Massachusetts Press.

———. 1986. "As the Crow Flies [August 19, 1944]." In *Newspaper Columns. Vol. 1, Amsterdam News*, compiled and edited by H. Aptheker, 600–1. White Plains, NY: Kraus-Thomson.

———. 1997. *The Correspondence of W. E. B. Du Bois. Vol. 3, Selections 1944–1963.* Pbk. ed. with corrections. Compiled and edited by H. Aptheker. Amherst: University of Massachusetts Press.

———. 2005. *W. E. B. Du Bois on Asia: Crossing the World Color Line.* Edited by B. Mullen and C. Watson. Jackson: University Press of Mississippi.

———. 2006. "Die Negerfrage in den Vereinigten Staaten" (The Negro Question in the United States). "W. E. B. Du Bois and the Question of Another World." Translated by Joseph Fracchia. Special Issue, *CR: New Centennial Review* 6, no. 3 (Autumn): 241–90.

———. 2010. "The Afro-American." *Journal of Transnational American Studies* 2, no. 1. http://escholarship.org/uc/item/2pm9g4q2.

———. 2012a. "Chapter 16—Jones in Japan." In "Toward a New Parallax: Or, Japan—in Another Traversal of the Trans-Pacific." Special issue, *CR: New Centennial Review* 12, no. 1 (Spring): 257–74.

———. 2012b. "Chapter 17—Jones Looks Back on China." In "Toward a New Parallax: Or, Japan—in Another Traversal of the Trans-Pacific." Special issue, *CR: New Centennial Review* 12, no. 1 (Spring): 275–90.

———. 2012c. "The Meaning of Japan (1937)." "Toward a New Parallax: Or, Japan—in Another Traversal of the Trans-Pacific." Special issue, *CR: New Centennial Review* 12, no. 1 (Spring): 233–56.

———. 2015a. "The Afro-American." In *The Problem of the Color Line at the Turn of the Twentieth Century: The Essential Early Essays*, compiled and edited by N. D. Chandler, 33–50. New York: Fordham University Press.

———. 2015b. "The Development of a People." In *The Problem of the Color Line at the Turn of the Twentieth Century: The Essential Early Essays* compiled and edited by N. D. Chandler, 243–270. New York: Fordham University Press.

———. 2015c. "Die Negerfrage in den Vereinigtin Staaten (The Negro Question in the United States) (1906)." In *The Problem of the Color Line at the Turn of the Twentieth Century: The Essential Early Essays*. Compiled and edited by N. D. Chandler, 285–338. New York: Fordham University Press.

———. 2015d. "The Present Outlook for the Dark Races of Mankind." In *The Essential Early Essays: Writings by W. E. B. Du Bois at the Turn of the Twentieth Century*, compiled and edited by N. D. Chandler, 111–137. New York: Fordham University Press.

———. 2015e. *The Problem of the Color Line at the Turn of the Twentieth Century: The Essential Early Essays*. Compiled and edited by N. D. Chandler. New York: Fordham University Press.

Du Bois, W. E. B., and Isabel Eaton. 1973. *The Philadelphia Negro: A Social Study*. Edited by Herbert Aptheker. Millwood, NY: Kraus Thomson.

Eschenbach, Wolfram von. 1980. *Parzival*. Translated by Arthur Thomas Hatto. Harmondsworth, UK: Penguin Books.

Evans, Grant, Chris Hutton, and Kuah Khun Eng, eds. 2000. *Where China Meets Southeast Asia: Social and Cultural Change in the Border Regions*. New York: St. Martin's Press.

Fanon, Frantz. 1961. *Les damnés de la terre*. Paris: F. Maspero.

Ferguson, James. 2006. *Global Shadows: Africa in the Neoliberal World Order*. Durham, NC: Duke University Press.

Fisk Jubilee Singers. 1955. *The Gold and Blue Album*. John W. Work, dir. New York: Folkways Records.

———. 1997. *Swing Low, Sweet Chariot. Fisk Jubilee Singers Vol. 1 (1909–1911)*. Galloway, Scotland: Document Records.

Foucault, Michel. 1973. *The Order of Things: An Archaeology of the Human Sciences*. New York: Vintage.

Freud, Sigmund. (1900) 1965. *The Interpretation of Dreams*. Translated by James Strachey. New York: Avon.

Gallicchio, Marc S. 2000. *The African American Encounter with Japan and China: Black Internationalism in Asia, 1895–1945*. Chapel Hill, NC: University of North Carolina.

Galvão, António. 1601. *The Discoueries of the World from Their First Originall vnto the Yeere of Our Lord 1555. Briefly Written in the Portugall Tongue by Antonie Galuano, Gouernour of Ternate, the Chiefe Island of the Malucos: Corrected, Quoted, and Now Published in English by Richard Hakluyt, Sometimes Student of Christ Church in Oxford*. Translated and edited by R. Hakluyt. Londin: Eliot's Court Press.

———. 1731. *Tratado dos descobrimentos antigos, e modernos, feitos até a Era de 1550 com os nomes particulares das pessoas que os fizeraõ: E em que tempos, e as suas alturas, e dos desuairados caminhos por onde a pimenta, e especiaria veyo da India as nossas partes; obra certo muy notavel, e copiosa (Treatise of discoveries ancient, and modern, from their first origins to the year 1550, with the particular names of those who made them: In what season, and in what latitude, and the uncommon routes by which pepper and spices came from India to our parts; a work certainly very remarkable and copious)*. Lisbon, Portugal: Officina Ferreiriana.

Geck, Martin. 2013. A Bedtime Story with Dire Consequences. In *Richard Wagner: A Life in Music*, translated by Stewart Spencer, 270–344. Chicago, IL: University of Chicago Press.

Gilroy, Paul. 1993a. *The Black Atlantic: Modernity and Double Consciousness*. Cambridge, MA: Harvard University Press.

———. 1993b. " 'Cheer the Weary Traveller': W. E. B. Du Bois, Germany and the Politics of (Dis)placement." In *The Black Atlantic Modernity and Double Consciousness*, 111–45. Cambridge, MA: Harvard University Press.

Gladney, Dru C. 2004. *Dislocating China: Reflections on Muslims, Minorities, and Other Subaltern Subjects*. Chicago, IL: University of Chicago Press.

Gordon, Lewis R. 2008. *An Introduction to Africana Philosophy*. New York: Cambridge University Press.

Guha, Ranajit 1997. "Colonialism in South Asia: A Dominance without Hegemony and Its Historiography." In *Dominance without Hegemony: History and Power in Colonial India*, 1–99. Cambridge, MA: Harvard University Press.

Hall, Stuart 1980. "Race, Articulation, and Societies Structured in Dominance." In *Sociological Theories: Race and Colonialism*. Paris: Unesco.

Hardt, Michael, and Antonio. Negri. 2000. *Empire*. Cambridge, MA: Harvard University Press.

———. 2004. *Multitude: War and Democracy in the Age of Empire*. New York: Penguin Press.

———. 2009. *Commonwealth*. Cambridge, MA: Belknap Press of Harvard University Press.

Hartman, Sadiya V. 1997. *Scenes of Subjection: Terror, Slavery, and Self-making in Nineteenth-Century America*. New York: Oxford University Press.

Harvey, David. 2006. *Spaces of Global Capitalism: Towards a Theory of Uneven Geographical Development*. London, New York: Verso.

Hilferding, Rudolf. 1981. *Finance Capital: A Study of the Latest Phase of Capitalist Development*. Edited by Tom B. Bottomore. Translated by Morris Watnick and Sam Gordon. London: Routledge & Kegan Paul.

Hobson, John Atkinson. 1905. *Imperialism: A Study*. Rev. ed. London: A. Constable.

Holt, Thomas C. 1990. Explaining Abolition. *Journal of Social History* 24, no. 2 (Winter): 371–78.

———. 1992. *The Problem of Freedom: Race, Labor, and Politics in Jamaica and Britain, 1832–1938*. Baltimore: Johns Hopkins University Press.

Horne, Gerald. 2004. *Race War! White Supremacy and the Japanese Attack on the British Empire*. New York: New York University Press.

James, C. L. R. 1972. Interview. In *Kas-kas; Interviews with Three Caribbean Writers in Texas: George Lamming, C. L. R. James [and] Wilson Harris*, edited by Ian Munro and Reinhard Sander. Austin: African and Afro-American Research Institute, University of Texas at Austin.

———. 1989. *The Black Jacobins: Toussaint L'Ouverture and the San Domingo Revolution*. New York: Vintage Books.

Jameson, Fredric. 2009. *Valences of the Dialectic*. London: Verso.

———. 2019. *Allegory and Ideology*. London: Verso.

Judy, Ronald A. T. 1993. *(Dis)forming the American Canon: African-Arabic Slave Narratives and the Vernacular*. Minneapolis: University of Minnesota Press.

Kant, Immanuel. 1992. "Dreams of a Spirit-seer Elucidated by Dreams of Metaphysics (1766)." In *Theoretical Philosophy, 1755–1770*, edited and translated by D. Walford, in collaboration with R. Meerbote, 301–60. Cambridge, UK; New York: Cambridge University Press.

———. 1998. *Critique of Pure Reason*. Edited and translated by Paul Guyer and Allen W. Wood. New York: Cambridge University Press.

———. 2000. *Critique of the Power of Judgment*. Edited by Paul Guyer. Translated by Paul Guyer and Eric Matthews. New York: Cambridge University Press.

———. 2007. "On the Use of Teleological Principles in Philosophy (1788)." Translated by Günter Zöller. In *Anthropology, History, and Education*, edited and translated by Robert B. Louden and Günter Zöller, 195–218. New York: Cambridge University Press.

Karatani, Kojin. 2003. *Transcritique: On Kant and Marx*. Translated by Sabu Kohso. Cambridge, MA: MIT Press.

Klein, Herbert. S. 1999. *The Atlantic Slave Trade*. New York: Cambridge University Press.

Koh, Jennifer, with R. Larry Todd. 2016. "Talking Music: Jennifer Koh." Duke Performances and Forum for Scholars & Publics, March 1, 2016. Video, 1:07. https://trinity.duke.edu/videos/talking-music-jennifer-koh.

Lach, Donald F. 1965. *Asia in the Making of Europe: Volume I: The Century of Discovery, Book One*. 4 vols. Chicago, IL: University of Chicago Press.

Lenin, Vladimir I. 1964. "Imperialism: The Highest Stage of Capitalism." Vol. 1. In *Selected Works*, vol. 1, 667–766. Moscow, Russia: Progress Publishers.

Lewis, David L. 2000. *W. E. B. Du Bois: The Fight for Equality and the American Century, 1919–1963*. New York: H. Holt.

———. 2002. Racism in the Service of Civil Rights: Du Bois in Germany, Cuba, and Japan, 1936–37. *Black Renaissance* 4, no. 1 (Spring): 8.

Marx, Karl 1977. *Capital: A Critique of Political Economy*. Vol. 1. Translated by B. Fowkes, introduction by E. Mandel. New York: Vintage.

McGann, Karen et al. 2019. *Africa's Great Civilizations*. San Francisco: PBS. (Film).

Mezzadra, Sandro. 2010. Introduzione. In *Sulla linea del colore: Razza e democrazia negli Stati Uniti e nel mondo*, by W. E. B. Du Bois, edited by Sandro Mezzadra and translated by Francisco Salvini, Marco Santoro, Sandro Mezzadra, and Chiara Scardoni, 7–102. Bologna, Italy: Società editrice il Mulino.

———. 2011. "The Topicality of Prehistory: A New Reading of Marx's Analysis of 'So-called Primitive Accumulation.' " Translated by Arianna Bove. *Rethinking Marxism* 23, no. 3 (July).

Moten, Fred. 2003. *In the Break: The Aesthetics of the Black Radical Tradition*. Minneapolis: University of Minnesota Press.

———. 2008. "Black Op." *PMLA* 123, no. 5: 1743–47.

Moss, Alford A., Jr. 1981. "Beginnings." In *The American Negro Academy: Voice of the Talented Tenth*, 35–57. Baton Rouge: Louisiana State University Press.

Mudimbe, Valentin Y. 1988. *The Invention of Africa Gnosis, Philosophy, and the Order of Knowledge*. Bloomington: Indiana University Press.

Mullen, Bill V. 2004. "W. E. B. Du Bois's Afro-Asian Fantasia." In *Afro-Orientalism*, 1–42. Minneapolis, Minnesota: University of Minnesota Press.

———. 2005. "Introduction: Crossing the World Color Line." In *W. E. B. Du Bois on Asia: Crossing the World Color Line*, edited by Bill Mullen and Cathryn Watson. Jackson: University Press of Mississippi.

Obama, Barack Hussein, Jr. 2016. "Text of President Obama's Speech in Hiroshima, Japan [Transcription]." *New York Times*. https://www.nytimes.com/2016/05/28/world/asia/text-of-president-obamas-speech-in-hiroshima-japan.html.

Outlaw, Lucius T. 1996. *On Race and Philosophy*. New York: Routledge.

Pomeranz, Kenneth 2000. *The Great Divergence: China, Europe, and the Making of the Modern World Economy*. Princeton, NJ: Princeton University Press.

Pope, Jeremy W. 2014. *The Double Kingdom under Taharqo: Studies in the History of Kush and Egypt, c. 690–864 BC*. Leiden, the Netherlands: Brill Academic Publishers.

Robeson, Paul 1991. "Go Down Moses." In *The Power and the Glory*. New York: Legacy—Columbia Records.

Robinson, Cedric J. [1983] 2000a. *Black Marxism: The Making of the Black Radical Tradition*. Foreword by Robin D. G. Kelley. Chapel Hill, NC: University of North Carolina Press.

———. [1983] 2000b. "Racial Capitalism: The Nonobjective Character of Capitalist Development. In *Black Marxism: The Making of the Black Radical Tradition*, foreword by Robin D. G. Kelley, 9–28. Chapel Hill, NC: University of North Carolina Press.

Rodney, Walter 1982. *How Europe Underdeveloped Africa*. Washington, DC: Howard University Press.

Rosenthal, Jean-Laurent and R. Bin Wong. 2011. *Before and beyond Divergence: The Politics of Economic Change in China and Europe*. Cambridge, MA: Harvard University Press.

Rossabi, Morris, ed. 2004. *Governing China's Multiethnic Frontiers*. Seattle: University of Washington Press.

Rothberg, Michael. 2001. "W. E. B. Du Bois in Warsaw: Holocaust Memory and the Color Line, 1949–1952." *Yale Journal of Criticism* 14, no. 1: 169–89.

Silva, Denise Ferreira da. 2007. *Toward a Global Idea of Race*. Minneapolis: University of Minnesota Press.

Spillers, Hortense J. 2003a. *Black, White, and in Color: Essays on American Literature and Culture*. Chicago, IL: University of Chicago Press.

———. 2003b. "The Crisis of the Negro Intellectual: A Post-Date." In *Black, White, and in Color: Essays on American Literature and Culture*, 428–70. Chicago, IL: University of Chicago Press.

Spivak, Gayatri Chakravorty. 1988. "Subaltern Studies: Deconstructing Historiography." In *Selected Subaltern Studies*, edited by R. Guha and G. C. Spivak, 3–32. New York: Oxford University Press.

Stanton, Lucia C. 2012. *"Those Who Labor for My Happiness": Slavery at Thomas Jefferson's Monticello*. Charlottesville: University of Virginia Press.

Stew. 2006. "Black Men Ski." Filmed February in Monterey, CA. TED video, 4:24. https://www.ted.com/talks/stew_black_men_ski/transcript.

Swinburne, Algernon C. 1904. "The Garden of Proserpine." In *The poems of Algernon Charles Swinburne. Vol. 1, Poems and Ballads, First Series*, 169–72. London: Chatto & Windus.

Taylor, Cecil. 1966. "Sound Structure of Subculture Becoming Major Breath/Naked Fire Gesture." Liner notes in *Unit structures*. Blue Note Records, BST 84237, LP.

Thurman, Kira. 2012. "Black Venus, White Bayreuth: Race, Sexuality, and the Depoliticization of Wagner in Postwar West Germany." *German Studies Review* 35, no. 3 (October): 607–26.

———. 2016. "Singing the Civilizing Mission in the Land of Bach, Beethoven, and Brahms: The Fisk Jubilee Singers in Nineteenth-century Germany." *Journal of World History* 27, no. 3 (September): 443–71.

———. 2019. "Performing Lieder, Hearing Race: Debating Blackness, Whiteness, and German Identity in Interwar Central Europe." *Journal of the American Musicological Society* 72, no. 3: 825–65.

Tsing, Anna L. 2005. *Friction: An Ethnography of Global Connection*. Princeton, NJ: Princeton University Press.

Vincent, William. 1807. "Section 26. Discoveries of the Portuguese." In *The Commerce and Navigation of the Ancients in the Indian Ocean*. 2 vols., 214–34. London: T. Cadell and W. Davies.

Wagner, Richard. 1987. *Lohengrin*. Georg Solti, conductor, with Jessye Norman et al. Konzertvereinigung Wiener Staatsopernchor, Wiener Philharmoniker. Decca Records, audio recording.

———. (ca. 1848) 1993. Libretto. Translated by Amanda Holden. In *Lohengrin*. London: J. Calder.

Wilderson, F. B. 2010. *Red, White & Black: Cinema and the Structure of U.S. Antagonisms*. Durham, NC: Duke University Press.

Wiencek, Henry. 2012. *Master of the Mountain: Thomas Jefferson and His Slaves*. New York: Farrar, Straus and Giroux.

Williams, Eric E. 1994. *Capitalism and Slavery*. Chapel Hill: University of North Carolina Press.

Wong, R. Bin. 1997. *China Transformed: Historical Change and the Limits of European Experience*. Ithaca, NY: Cornell University Press.

Žižek, Slavoj. 2006. *The Parallax View*. Cambridge, MA: MIT Press.

Index

Accra, Ghana, 106
Achaean League, 92
Adelson, Leslie, 37
Africa, xii, 5, 16–19, 50, 51–52, 55, 81, 116n8; Africa and Asia, 68; Algeria, 55; in America, 56; ancient Egypt, 17; Egypt, 50, 55; Libya, 55; Maurutania, 55; South Africa, 37; Tunisia, 55; Western Sahara, Saharawi eruption, 55
Africa as a region, ancient Kush, 92
African American musical tradition, 87
African American, 3; as example, 1, 3–5, 8, 9–16
African musician, from the Kinshasa Symphony Orchestra, 101
Afro-Asia, 50–51
Alantic slavery, 41
Alle Menschen, 125, 100. *See also* Beethoven, Ludwig van, *Symphony No. 9 in D Minor*
allegoresis, 88
allegory, double allegory, 94
Althusser, Louis, 40
America: European America, 57; and Japan, 114n3
American Civil War, 104, 105
American Negro Academy, 32, 108n4
American South, 90; Georgia coast, 95

Americas, as region: Brazil, 37; Caribbean, 5, 65, 81; Cuba, 36; Haiti, 72; Hawai'i, 36; Puerto Rico, 36; United States, 10, 36–38, 115n6; United States, the, 55–56
anagogical declaration in Du Bois's *Color and Democracy*, 87
Anderson, Marian, 96–97; 1939 performance at the Lincoln Memorial, 104–5
anorientation, 1
apocalypse of two world wars, 92
Aptheker, Herbert, 72, 116n10, 117
Arab countries, 101
Arrighi, Giovanni, 45–46, 55
Asia, 5, 24–28, 36; Asian century, idea of, 57; China, 10, 25, 37, 50–51, 55, 57; China, Manchuria, 25; China, Nanking massacre, 25; India, 10, 28, 37, 50; and Indian Ocean, 48; Indonesia, 10, 37; Japan, 5, 25–28, 37, 51, 57; Korea, 10, 26, 51; Korea, South Korea, 37; Okinawa (aka Rykūkyū Islands), 25; Pacific Rim, 48; Philippines, 10, 36; Vietnam, 10
Asia, as region: China, 102, 110–12n12, 113–14n3; India, 111n12, 112n1; Japan, 102, 110–12n12,

Go Down Moses!, 104–6; and
  spirituals, 87. *See also* spirituals
Gonçalves, Antonio, 112–13n2. *See
  also* Galvão, António
Gordon, Lewis Ricardo, 57, 116n7
Great Depression, 43
Great March on Washington, 103
Great Pacific War, 67
Guha, Ranajit, 40–41

Hall, Stuart, 109n6
Hamer, Fannie Lou, 56
Harcourt, Brace, 61, 72. *See also*
  Du Bois, W. E. B., *Color and
  Democracy*
Hardt, Michael, 45, 107n3, 109n6
Harney, Stefano, ix
Hartman, Saidiya, 116n7
Harvey, David, 45
Hebrew tradition, 104
Hegel, G. W. F., 107n2
Hilferding, Rudolf, 43
Hiroshima, 67. *See also* nuclear weapons
historial, 80, 92
historical world, 94–95. *See also*
  allegory
historicity, 104; and Africa, 67; as
  making a way out of no way,
  78; modern capitalization and
  enslavement, 76–77; modern
  enslavement, 70–71; modern
  enslavement and its aftermath, 81;
  modern historicity: the fifteenth
  century through twentieth century,
  67; as sense of world, 71; as source
  of values as ideals, 71
historiography, 69
Hitler, Adolf, 96
Hobson, John A., 43
Holt, Thomas C., 109n6
Holy Alliance, 92. *See also* a "worldwide"
  confederation of nations and states

Holy Roman Empire, 92. *See also* a
  "worldwide" confederation of nations
  and states
hope, 85
Horne, Gerald, 107n1
Huebsch, B. W., 72. *See also* Viking
  Press
humanism, 65
Hutton, Christopher, 116n10

immigration, protest of policies in the
  United States (2006), 115n6
imperialism, xii, 49, 111n12,
  113–14n3; as European rivalry,
  41; as reconciled with aristocracy
  and despotism, 42, 43; workers as
  investors in, 42–43
"In Fernem Land" in Wagner's
  Lohengrin, 91
internationalism, liberal, 111n12
Irene Diggs, assistant to Du Bois on
  The World and Africa, 74
Israel, 101

James, C. L. R., 109n6
Jameson, Fredric, x, 88, 94, 107n2
Japan Black Studies Association
  (Kokujin Kenkyu no Kai), ix
Jefferson, Thomas, and mortgaging of
  enslaved labor, 79–80
Jewish, 104
Jewish tradition and family descent,
  Judaism, 63
John Brown, 105
Jones, Jennie, in *The Souls of Black
  Folk*, 89; in "Of the Coming of
  John," 95
Jones, John, in *The Souls of Black Folk*,
  93; in "Of the Coming of John,"
  95
Judaic premise, 104
Judy, Ronald A. T., 115n7